Latinas in
FINANCES

Changing the financial narrative one Latina at a time

IMELDA RODRÍGUEZ

Latinas in FINANCES

This book is a compilation of stories from numerous people who have each contributed a chapter and is designed to provide inspiration to our readers.

It is sold with the understanding that the publisher and the individual authors are not engaged in the rendering of psychological, legal, accounting or other professional advice. The content and views in each chapter are the sole expression and opinion of its author and not necessarily the views of Fig Factor Media, LLC.

For more information, contact:
Fig Factor Media, LLC | www.figfactormedia.com
Latinas in Finances | www.latinasinfinances.com

Cover Design by DG Marco Alvarez
Layout by LDG Juan Manuel Serna Rosales

Printed in the United States of America

ISBN: 978-1-957058-16-0
Library of Congress Control Number: 2022922100

To God be the Glory!

To my daughter, Valeria Zoe, for being my everyday inspiration and to my mother, Edna Rodriguez, for supporting me every single mile of my dream. To my aunt Angelica Rodriguez, we are family and together we are stronger. We are "Las Rodriguez".

TABLE OF CONTENTS

ACKNOWLEDGMENTS

My heart is filled with so many THANKS.

Thank you, God, for planting this dream in my heart.

I would like to thank everyone in the Fig Factor Media team and, of course, Jackie Camacho-Ruiz for believing in me not to run but to fly for this mission.

Thank you to Izar Olivares for your outstanding dedication to making this book happen from A to Z.

I am very thankful to every single co-author/co-dreamer for believing in me and in this dream of leaving a legacy to the future generations. We will see them in the important financial conversations.

Gratitude to our future generations who are and have always been our most important inspiration, this acknowledgment is for you. You are the reason we do this work.

FOREWORD

There are nearly five million Hispanic-owned businesses in the United States that contribute more than 800 billion dollars to the American economy annually and more than 300,000 Hispanic-owned, employer businesses located across all fifty states and the District of Columbia. There are over two million Latina-owned businesses in the country, a growth of more than 87 percent since 2007, according to the National Women's Business Council.

Latinas in Finances: Changing the Financial Narrative One Latina at a Time is a testament to Latinas given with heart and emotion as these ladies tell of their struggles and the lessons they have learned. The Latino market has a spending power of over two-and-a-half trillion dollars. Latinas are not just part of the market; they are the most exciting part of it—they are the mainstream market. These Latinas are helping to fuel the U.S. economy. But what you may not know is that Latinas are leading in this new business world. Latinas are, in short, the future.

These are facts and figures and data that will decide your financial future and mine.

Latin culture is a "we", not a "me" culture. We see society as a reflection of our family or community. Latinos as people respect feelings, and many times guide us. We overemphasize feelings. We factor in feelings and emotions in our language is gender-based. We see the world by gender. Words come alive in pronouns of *el* and *la*. Latinas are winning in finance because they are leaning into their emotions, they are titans in finance because Latinas are using their culture. They are not hiding their culture; they are "leaning into it."

Latinas have a great love for family. When my mother went to work in the morning, she did not dream of things or possessions; she dreamed of the opportunity to give her family what they did not have. She dreamed of a home in a better neighborhood with schools that gave us a better opportunity.

There were three Latino families in our middle-class neighborhood. Other than my own, there were the Ochoa's and the Vargas. They, like mine, were raised with Latino values and culture. Elena Ochoa and Juan Vargas grew up with me. Ochoa eventually became the first Latina astronaut and Vargas the first Latino congressman. In my city, all the Latinos sacrificed to live in that community. All of us learned the sacrifice and hard work it takes to achieve something. Who did we learn it from? We learned it from the examples our families gave us every day. Our parents and culture value hard work. We have never been scared of hard work or the lack of work because if there was not a job available, we would create one. In fact, not only do we value hard work, we look for it. Maybe that is the contribution immigrants make but we are complex because some of our people were here for hundreds of years. My grandfather did not cross a border because there was none. It's our work ethic we value and celebrate.

The second thing we value in our culture is self-sacrifice. We are not scared to work hard. I would witness that every day when I would watch my father go to a job at six in the morning and witness my mom leave for her job at nine after she fed her children. They worked hard and long hours, at times from early morning to late at night. At my Boy Scout troop or Little League practice, I would not have my mom or dad there but I knew where my mom and dad were and what they doing. They were working, working to feed us. Dreaming is another aspect of the culture. We dream and we aspire to work on our dreams. We are Don Quixote—we dreamed of the impossible dream. Don Quixote was our mystical knight on a wild romantic quest. Don Quixote was also our parents. They loved us and that's why they worked. We were their "Impossible Dream," like the man of la Mancha who dreamed an impossible dream. Many of these women share in their stories about dreams that although sometimes their dreams seem impossible but the fact that they look impossible only spurned these ladies to try them. The book is a love letter to our mothers and the families they raised and the businesses they started

"To dream the impossible dream
To fight the unbeatable foe
To bear with unbearable sorrow
And to run where the brave dare not go
To right the unrightable wrong
And to love pure and chaste from afar
To try when your arms are too weary
To reach the unreachable star

This is my quest
To follow that star
No matter how hopeless
No matter how far
To fight for the right
Without question or pause
To be willing to march, march into Hell
For that Heavenly cause."

—Richard Kiley

Yes, we honor these traits—love, work, sacrifice—and this book will show those same values in a celebratory way. These Latina stories are written to inspire us all. Best of all, you do not have to be a Latina to enjoy this book. All you have to do is have a heart. I highly recommend this book to anyone who needs to learn about Latinas in business or learn about opportunities in this two-and-a-half-trillion-dollar market or simply be inspired. If those are the stories you like to read then this book is for you.

Viva la Mujer. The future is here and it is Latina.

Rick Najera
Award-winning screenwriter, actor, director, producer, author, playwright, coach and national speaker.

INTRODUCTION

It all started with my heart knowing that *Latinas in Finances* will happen at some point. I noticed how the Latinas in series started and from the very beginning, I knew that it was going to be a reality. I contacted Jaqueline Camacho-Ruiz to add my name to the list a co-author. Before I knew it, I was appointed as the person with all the skills and knowledge to run a project like this. I said yes without hesitation and, to be completely honest, I failed as simple as that. Three months after many meetings and conversations with potential collaborators, I end up with nothing. Months passed and I couldn't see the reasons.

One day, I stood in the middle of a room and asked myself for the multiple reasons, until it click very hardly to my heart with Proverbs 3: 5-6:

> Trust in the Lord with all your heart
> and lean not on your own understanding;
> in all your ways submit to him,
> and he will make your paths straight.

The answer was in front of me. I was leaning on my own understanding and the results were obviously clear. This time, I leaned and trusted in the Lord to guide me and I told Him: "If you really want me here, you will lead me and you will make the path straight." I opened the application for an author to apply, three months after we were eighteen authors ready to start writing our stories. I could never imagine the results, but I knew that this time I was not alone and that itself made such a huge difference. As we are preparing for the book to be ready, I can already envision Volume two.

The story of each author has many ups and downs. Who said that life is a straight line? But every time you read those stories you will get the inspiration to move up or forward. You will be able to see yourself in these stories of adversity and success. The best part? They are Latinas, and our lives are not that far from whatever situation you are going through. We are here to uplift you while you are living your unique story.

This is not just a book but a movement aiming to build generational wealth and to increase the percentage of Latinas in finance. There are many financial topics that we need to address, and the list could be endless. But we are the ones standing up to speak up: Wage gap, racial gap, financial instability, generational wealth, gender pay gap, equity, diversity, inclusion, access to mainstream benefits, assets acquisition, high interest lender services, insufficient credit history, low-to-none credit scores, student loan debt, unfavorable financing options, predatory lending practices, low-to-none savings, unable to invest, check cashing services, limited knowledge and access to information, limited access to credit building opportunities, low wages, gentrification, unbanked, underbanked, you name it.

Together, we will be part of the solutions, each of us has been working independently to support our communities one way or another. Today, we decided to break the stereotype that all the Latinas do not know how to work together. We are working together, and this is our way to tell the world that there is always a way to extend our hand to the ones in need. Today, the ones in need are not always the ones that need something material. There are many that need something else, like coaching, guidance, support, teaching, and education. Together, we will be able to change the narrative one Latina at a time. I truly believe that if we invest in one Latina a whole household will change for better. We just need to work together instead of solos, the more the better. This is our time, and we are the future.

Latinas are vital to the U.S. economy and critically influential as voters. Latinos contribute 2.6 trillion dollars to the U.S. economy in 2019, yet Latinas still earn fifty-five cents for every dollar earned by white, non-Hispanic men. It will take a Latina twenty-three months to earn what a white men earn in twelve. The average white, non-Hispanic male in the United States working full time and part time earns about an average $50,624 a year, according to analysis of U.S. Census Bureau data from Justice for Migrant Women. Meanwhile, the average amount of Money a Latina makes in a year is just $25,312, according to that analysis. COVID-19 has had a particularly devastating impact on Latinas: 21 percent of Latinas lost jobs in the early days of the pandemic, nearly a quarter of Latinas do not have access to health insurance, and only 16 percent could work from home. We need change and we need it now, there is no more time to expect for something to happen.

On top of that, many Latino families feel the pressure of supporting multi-generations like their aging parents and family members located overseas, while taking care of immediate family. Simply imagine splitting the dollar in many fractions. Yes, we do love our families and we worry about their needs. Our values and culture are very important. Generational wealth and investments can feel out of reach when we do not even see ourselves being represented in important financial conversations. Splitting the check in many portions will not support the long-term goals.

A 2020 study on low-income Latinas and the relationship between financial stress and mental health found that we are less likely to receive mental health services than non-Hispanic whites or African-American women. In an earlier study, Latinos attributed interpersonal problems and economic strain as significant factors affecting their mental health and described a lack of coping strategies and emotional support systems.

There are many obstacles to overcome, but nothing is impossible. By working together, we will be able to amplify the stories of diverse, unheard, and underrepresented Latinas. Collectively, we will be able to build and shift the history and the statistics. This is a call to action, together we can change the future because we are the future!

Imelda Rodriguez

MONEY MATTERS WHILE
GROWING UP

IMELDA
RODRIGUEZ

*"Any amount of money in your hand gives you the
opportunity to retain or to multiply."*

I grew up between two cultures, Mexico and the United States—bilingual, bicultural and biliterate. Both cultures gave me everything I am now. Money has been part of my whole life. I clearly remember growing up in my family's business, El Instituto Administrativo y Comercial Fenix (The Administrative and Commercial Institute Fenix). As the daughter of the principal and owner, any basic need of mine was covered. I remember having everything, and not one but two or more of some things (food, shelter, school supplies, clothing, etc.). You name it, and I had it. Even during the Día de Reyes (Epiphany), my mom used to take me to the toy store to choose my own toys. I was told not to select just one toy, but to fill a cart. That not being enough, she would get a second cart and fill that one with toys for me (the ones she wanted for me). My mother grew up having all her needs covered. Being the third woman in the family that would carry the legacy was not easy, but as the daughter of the second woman, "La Prin" as everyone knew her, it was easy. She did not have to manage any budget. She just needed to ask for money. During her adulthood, when she was the one managing her money, I know she had a section on her invisible budget, called travel expenses. She was traveling all the time, in the state, out of the state, and even internationally. Souvenirs would appear in my bedroom as surprises from her trips. At one point I started selling them to my classmates. Of course, once I started seeing the money coming into my savings account, I saw the beginning of my entrepreneurial adventure. Sales are very natural and they always bring money to your pockets.

I was about five years old when my Aunt Angie was teaching me to set up a table outside of the classrooms for the students to buy candies from us. Unbelievably, the students were buying candies from us (the daughter and the little sister of the principal). Later, we pivoted the business by adding fruit with chili powder, and magazines and books for rent. Right away, I noticed that my accounting skills were very precise. My budget covered all the expenses, profits were constantly coming in, and my numbers were never red.

Later, when I was about six years old, a friend of my mom's,

Norma Cedeño, a Latina business owner, had a bazaar and a second stream of income coming in by the name of Arabela. Norma saw my talent at that youthful age. She gave me all the tools I needed to start—receipts, inventory, bags, etc. I was ready to start selling, and you know, I did. I did it very well. The business kept growing. So, I added more merchandise, like shoes with a catalog, magazines, movies rental, and anything that clients requested. At that point in my life, I understood that sales were going to become part of my life.

Life was not easy during the year 1994. Mexico's economy crashed during the time of President Carlos Salinas de Gortari. My life was impacted by that financial crash. I experienced too many changes: new schools, new homes, new classmates. The society in Mexico is exceptionally good at showing you the economic class that you belong in–low, medium, or high. Life keeps showing me that not everything will last forever. It is crucial for everyone to have multiple streams of income, that any way to secure assets and your family will never be an expense but an investment because, honestly, there is no way to know what could happen at any moment.

GENERATIONS MATTER

Being the fourth woman entrepreneur in my family has challenges and opportunities. My great-grandmother, Guadalupe Olvera Argandar (1900-1973), was a pioneer back in those years, a leader among women. In 1947, at a time when businesses were for men only, she opened a school at the age of forty-seven. Being a woman entrepreneur was not easy. She genuinely cared about education for her future generations. She blended her passion and made a profit from it. Under her leadership, the school continued to grow in number of students and profit. Twenty-six years later, the business was positioned very well in the city and the state. My great-grandmother passed away, and her legacy for my grandmother, Imelda Guadalupe Ramirez Olvera (1937-1981), also known as "La Prin," was for her to continue, to increase, and to multiply wealth. Students were coming from everywhere because the school delivered quality education. Teachers were held to a high standard. My grandmother was very pushy; she wanted her students to represent well. Whether they were working or doing their internship, she wanted to hear excellent feedback about them. Obviously, her life's work had a due date, and that year was 1981. She died suddenly and unexpectedly at the youthful age of forty-four. Her term as the principal was only eight years. My mother was the oldest of three siblings, and she had to take over when she was only twenty-two years old. Can you imagine a twenty-two year old appointed to manage a huge business legacy with its assets, wealth, and decisions, as well as the matriarchy of a family, both direct and indirect? It was not easy; I can guarantee it. Responsibilities like those are the ones that shake the confidence of the person suddenly responsible for deciding the next step. My mother was able to continue as the third woman in command, serving as the principal of the school for twenty years. Without hesitation I can say that she did amazingly well. She immersed herself in the educational business, preparing people to be good citizens in any area they represented. She is alive today, and she left everything for her little brother to continue with the Fenix mission.

THE LEGENDARY PHOENIX

"Fenix" (Phoenix-Féniks) in classical mythology was a unique bird that lived for five or six centuries in the Arabian desert, burning itself on a funeral pyre and rising from the ashes with renewed youth to live through another cycle. Now I know that the name my great grandmother thought of for the business was just the right one, as I continue to see the cycle repeat. It is extremely important to prepare your next generation. Do not take anything for granted, we do not know the future, and we do not know the time we have here on earth. For the cycle to continue, it is important to educate and to train your kids to continue and to increase their wealth. They will not do it just because they are the next generation. One thing I know for fact: any time there are siblings, and money without a will, there will be family fights over the assets. Those arguments can hurt multiple generations. I experienced every piece of that, and I will not recommend it to anyone. The best investments anyone can make are wills and life insurance.

EDUCATIONS MATTERS

Education runs in my DNA, as you can tell. From an incredibly early age I knew I was going to become an entrepreneur, so I went to school for business administration.

Honestly, do not ask me why, but I knew that I was going to be la dueña (the business owner). So, every class I took since high school was related to business, marketing, and finance. You always keep getting ready for whatever you want to become. It takes time and effort, but I keep the focus point on the target. I remember myself running around the classroom, the patio, the offices, and I kept telling myself that I was going to transform the school into a mall. The plan was to remodel the school into a plaza and to rent every single space to make a profit from it. I even remember the name; The Green Plaza. You can always dream about the future, but education will shape you and will provide all the tools that you need to achieve your dreams. Your age is not important as there is no law or rule for you to enroll in school or for you to continue or even to finish what you started. Do what you must do and do it well. Believe me, you will not regret it. Life will give you different situations that could stop the normal flow but if you keep moving at any rhythm, you will get to the finish line. Every class, training, certification, or coaching session will lead you to the next level.

Latinas have made considerable progress in education in the last two decades. If we continue to increase those numbers, we could see higher earnings and lower unemployment. While education attainments narrow the wage gap, Latinas with advanced degrees still earn less than white, non-Hispanic men with bachelor's degrees. Education is not a panacea for structural inequality, but we do need to do our part.

FINANCE AND BUSINESS MATTERS

Latino small business owners are the fastest-growing group of entrepreneurs in the United States. The Stanford University Research Initiative study found that Latino-owned businesses contribute about 500 billion dollars to the economy in annual sales. The same report also indicated that Latino-owned businesses employ more than three million people. All those statistics happening even with all the barriers that Latinos encounter: Less generational wealth than white people, income gap, gender gap, wage gap, lower credit scores, discrimination, low or non-access to capital, and high interest rates, are among the obstacles. Latinos contributed $2.6 trillion to the U.S. economy in 2019, yet Latinas earn fifty-five cents for every dollar earned by white, non-Hispanic men. COVID-19 has had a particularly devastating impact on Latinas: 21 percent of Latinas lost jobs in the early days of the pandemic, a quarter of Latinas do not have access to health insurance, and only 16 percent can work from home. We are particularly important to the U.S. economy, and if we continue opening and maintaining business in good standing, we will be able to not only change the statistics, but leave wealth and financial legacy to our future generations.

One thing I know for sure is that investing and generational wealth looks out of reach because we are not seeing ourselves represented in the financial field. Representation is especially important, as not everyone understands that in our households, we take care of our parents while raising our own kids and, often, we also send money overseas to our extended family. Being a businessperson brings more tasks to the to-do list. We take care of our family, while holding a full-time job and taking care of the small business at the same time. As Latinas, we are always thinking about better ways to make our world better. Businesses are there because something was missing, and we found the solution.

Coaching Vida started back in December 2019, three months after COVID-19 hit the entire world. Yes, I had to work a regular full-time job as I knew the business would not cover my expenses. It is during these crises that creativity comes in handy to pivot and find ways to move forward to the next level, and sometimes just to maintain what I had. Later, I was able to connect with other businesses and not-for-profits that hire our life and financial coaching services. Things will not happen overnight and working hard is necessary. As a business owner, I am the first one and the last one at the same time, the one that opens and the one that closes the door every day. As a Latina, I am not afraid of demanding work, and I even look for ways to support others. I can see myself involved with not-for-profit organizations that are doing something for the community; the ones supporting the children, the ones going through domestic violence, the ones in need of basic things like food or clothing, the youth, the families. No matter how much time in life we have, there is never enough time to help everyone.

The inspiration for Latinas in Finances came during COVID-19. I know that when your passion and your professional background collide, the explosion can become something pure and strong. In this case, a book will last forever, and the future generations will be able to read our stories without us being physically in front of them. Follow your passion, your DNA, your line of succession, your history, your legacy and, more than anything, what God is telling you to do. In everything you do, put God first, second and last.

"In everything you do, put God first, and he will direct you and crown your efforts with success." (Proverbs 3:6)

The best is yet to come.

MY FINANCE INSPIRATION

Today, more than ever, it is important for us as Latinas to expand our representation in this industry. We represent 10 percent of the U.S. population and the percentage is combined between management, administration, and finances. If we increase that percentage, we have a higher chance to be able to sit at the table and make major decisions in finance. Each of us represents our families, neighborhoods, communities, cities, states, and our countries. The importance of earning a seat at the table will change the financial narrative one Latina at a time and give us better opportunities to make sure that Latinas are forever represented in this industry.

I would like to ask you these questions:

1. What are you doing to learn and manage your own finances?
2. What are you doing to teach your family about the household's finances?

3. What would you do to become the best seller of your product or service?

Financial coaches and/or financial coaching resources:
1. Not-for-profit organizations in your own area—financial coaching
2. Local Initiatives Support Corporation (LISC)—Financial Opportunity Centers®
3. Financial Coaching Strategies by University of Wisconsin-Madison
4. Central New Mexico Community College Financial Coaching Training
5. Credit as an Asset Master Trainer Certification by Training Institute Credit Builders Alliance

CONNIE ALBAN-FRANCO

"I compare one part of my life to a video game: always running, always unlocking levels, but never finding peace. It was not until I found the right people in my life that doors began to unlock for me."

To my Luciano and my Fiorella. With God, everything is possible.

"What no eye has seen, what no ear has heard, and what no human mind has conceived the things God has prepared for those who love Him." 1 Corinthians 2:9

"Dad, I think I am going to pursue a career in finance." He nodded and said: "I think that is a great fit for you." This was one of the last conversations I had with my dad; he was picking me up from college. Fifteen years have gone by, and I repeat this

11

memory over and over because it is one of my treasures, one of my last and most clear memories of my dad.

I was born and raised in latitude zero, Quito, Ecuador, a place where peaceful people live in the middle of active volcanoes, enjoying an eternal spring. I must say, I had a pleasant childhood. I was a girl, raised traditionally in an all-girls private Catholic school. I loved learning and was thrilled to enroll in every extracurricular activity there was: dancing, French classes, speech contest, all the way to playing a role in the Model UN, which is a simulation of the United Nations General Assembly for high school students. I loved the fact that teenagers from the whole town would get together to discuss solutions to world inequality.

My plan was clear. I was going to enroll in a French university right after high school. I had the whole world in front of me. Things were nice, smooth, easy.

It was the morning of April 28, 2007. As I woke up, my mother told me my father hadn't come home from work the night before, and he was not answering his cell phone. This was the very first time something like this had happened. I thought to myself it was really weird, but I was sure my dad would answer the phone if I called him. I got up and walked towards my cell phone. Suddenly, the intercom rang. It was a lady asking if Mr. Gonzalo Alban lived there. I said yes. She said he'd had an accident and I had to come with her. I rushed to the first floor, thinking my dad was at the hospital and needed my help. When I opened the door, I saw a medium-sized brunette wearing all black from head to toe. Her face is blurry in my memory but I can still remember her presence. She came to tell me that my father had a car accident at the corner near our house; he had passed away. She was there to offer me her funeral services, as she was the owner of a local funeral home. I can still feel the pain I felt on that fateful day. It was so excruciating that I fell to my knees. The pain was so real that my chest started hurting. I do believe no one knows what pain is until you lose someone you love. I don't know how long I was there, but I had to get up. I had to give the news to my mother, my fourteen-year-old sister, and my seven-year-old brother. Gonzalo Jr., my little brother, somehow already knew what happened. He told me he had a dream about my dad having a car accident. In that dream he had hurt his leg and was telling jokes to my brother, as he usually did. I just think that was his way of saying goodbye.

That day my life changed. I found myself in front of a desk in a funeral home, not really understanding what was happening. What I remember is that they gave me an agreement to proceed with my father's funeral. I felt numb. I was about to sign a paper I didn't read, and I didn't care. I just wanted everything to end. It is on occasions like these that you value those friends who come to your aid. My friend, Daniela Bucheli, a law student at the time, prevented me from signing the document without her review. (A lesson that I keep with me: surround yourself with good people).

This was the event that changed my life forever. My real journey began here. At twenty-two years old, I had the weight of the world on my shoulders. At twenty-two, I learned what a mortgage is, and how to prepare a funeral, as well as how to face the legal system. I'd never felt so alone. I no longer had my protector.

My father was not a very demonstrative or affectionate man, but I understood that my father's way of loving us was to plan for the future through good financial planning. He used to say: "Always plan for the future. Look ahead." He was the first entrepreneur that I met. He started his appraisal company from zero. From him, I learned what it means to work long hours and to bring the laptop home on the weekends to meet clients' deadlines.

When he passed away, we were debt free. Among the assets my father left us, what became paramount, the key that opened my financial career, was LIFE INSURANCE. My father had life insurance! In the midst of so much pain and confusion, knowing that my father had life insurance was like having a life jacket in the middle of a shipwreck. Because of life insurance, I was able to finish my last year in college. My mother was not working at the time, and my two siblings were still fairly young. Life insurance gave us the financial freedom to put our whole life as we knew it in a bag and come to the United States of America.

A new chapter started in my life. I came to Chicago not knowing what was ahead for me. To be honest, it was not my choice. I feel like life pushed me somehow to come here. The Windy City was a city written in my destiny. Here I fell in love, got married, and had two amazing kids.

Migrating to a country that is not yours is very hard. The American dream, the one that you see in the movies, is far from reality. I knocked on many doors but few opened. I was too naïve. I thought I had financial education, but the reality is that the

USA has its own system. If you don't play by the rules, it will break you. It took me so many years, and so many tears, to learn the hard way how things are supposed to be done. I compare one part of my life to a video game: always running, always unlocking levels, but never finding peace. It was not until I found the right people in my life that doors began to unlock for me.

In my very first administration class, my teacher's opening phrase was: "The most important thing that an entrepreneur has is her team."

What a great truth. The people you surround yourself with have a direct influence on you. Not believing in myself and my abilities kept me trapped for many years in a job where I couldn't develop to my true potential. I wasted my talent in exchange for a secure salary. I settled for little. While my employer grew exponentially, I barely did. Having young kids and being a professional woman is extremely difficult. There aren't many working laws that protect you. I was not happy. I had a job, but no growth. There wasn't a purpose, I was just surviving.

MY FINANCE INSPIRATION

This was the point in my life when I was drained. I could not take it anymore. My intuition told me there was something else. I needed a change. So, I called Anna Harambasic, my old company's insurance agent. I asked her if I could work for her. I was not attracted to the insurance industry per se; I was motivated to work with Anna because of her work ethic and honesty—values that are not easy to find.

I planned to work in an administrative role. To my surprise, every day I learned something new. This job pushed me to investigate. I fell in love with insurance. So much information opened my eyes. The truth will set you free. Learning about insurance gave me knowledge about how the system works in the USA.

I recall the day that I was told that credit has a direct impact on the price of auto and property insurance. Finally, I understood what makes up an insurance rate. That day I promised myself that I would teach people how to lower their insurance rates. I would not let people go blind, as I did for so long. I needed to empower people and make sure they could make a good decision that fit their situation, knowing what options they had and the difference between coverages. I schedule consulting calls. I never assume my customers know it all. On the contrary, I want to make sure they feel they can ask me any question, and I start from the very basic terms. You would be surprised by how much misinformation there is when it comes to insurance, regardless of the person's background or level of education.

It was November 2019 when one of the agency customers walked through the door. She wanted to pay her business insurance. I am talking about an amazing, hard-working woman who started from nothing to owning her own cleaning company. I asked her if she had life insurance, and she looked at me, and with shame in her eyes, in a low broken tone of voice she said: "I don't have one. I don't have a Social Security number." I told her: "Don't worry, I can help you with your ITIN. Let's get you started." She smiled and applied for her permanent life insurance. She didn't know how much life insurance she should buy, and what options were out there, but she was eager to learn. This "business transaction" gave me peace, gave me happiness. I had finally found a way to make a living and help people. I had found my calling.

In my darkest times, life insurance was there for my family. I knew my brother and sister were able to continue to go to school. We were able to keep the house my dad built. This is my commitment. I will keep spreading life insurance awareness, as a form of wealth transfer and a form of leaving a legacy. I don't want anyone to lose someone they love and be in a difficult financial position that forces them to start a GoFundMe account to pay for a funeral.

I hate injustice and I hate when unscrupulous salespeople cheat honest people just to sell an insurance policy. I am not only a sales producer. My job is to teach insurance literacy. I am passionate about what I do. Insurance is the weapon that God has given me to fight for what is right, and to protect people's dreams. After 3.5 years, I have helped more than 300 families gain protection with life insurance.

While my life story is still being written, there is so much to learn. Follow your instincts. Try new things even if it is scary. Push yourself. The only race out there is the race against yourself. Set goals and pursue them daily. If you fall, that is okay, get back up again. When I started in this business a wise gentleman told me, "Whether you are an insurance agent or not, there's no halfway to doing anything in life." Surround yourself with people who push your limits, who teach you as well as inspire you. Find a mentor who will guide you in this journey. If you do, be grateful. People don't share their knowledge or wisdom easily.

I would not be who I am today without the support of my mentor, Anna, whom I love, respect, and admire. I am forever grateful to have met her. People will come to you if you honestly want to help them. If you decide to pursue a career in the insurance industry and you are an ethical, honest professional, you might become a lighthouse in the storm for others.

BIOGRAPHY

Connie has a beautiful family with Nano, her husband of more than a decade. Together they have a vibrant ten-year-old, Fiorella, and lionhearted seven-year-old, Luciano. Connie started her business career when she was fourteen years old with an Internship at DHL, followed by a second internship in the International Business MICIP–World Bank 4346 EC Project. When she was eighteen, she held her first job as an administrative assistant at IBM Ecuador while she pursued her Business Administration (BA) degree full time at the USFQ–Universidad San Francisco de Quito. Currently, Connie possesses property, casualty, and life licenses to practice insurance in Illinois and Wisconsin. Connie works as an insurance specialist at the Anna Harambasic Amfam Agency, recognized as the agency of the year in 2021 for District 815. Amfam–American Family Insurance Group, is the nation's thirteenth largest property/casualty insurance group, ranking No. 251 on the Fortune 500 list. At the same time, in 2022, Amfam earned a place on Ward Group nation's top fifty performing Life Insurance companies.

As part of Connie's commitment to empowering her community, she collaborates with the Women's Business Development Center (WBDC) as a guest speaker for the Startup, as well as the Scale-up programs, giving commercial insurance webinars to entrepreneurs. Moreover, in 2021, Connie collaborated with the National Association of Hispanic Real Estate Professionals (NAHREP), as part of the Philanthropy

Committee. In 2022, Connie continues collaborating as a member of the events committee with NAHREP Chicago in its pursuit to help more Hispanic families achieve homeownership in a sustainable way.

Connie Alban-Franco
calbanfr@amfam.com
(773) 794-9200
Facebook: @conniealbanfranco
Instagram: @connie.amfam
LinkedIn: Connie Alban-Franco

TAKING THE LEAP TO LATINA BUSINESS OWNER

ADRIANA GALVAN

"I want everyone to feel the same liberation when they are able to quit a toxic job, leave their cheating partner, or feel secure when they find out they are getting laid off. Adriana Talks Dinero, LLC is changing people's way of thinking about money, and it will change people's lives in the process. This is the legacy I am leaving behind for future generations, and my gift to the world."

LA CHINGONA WITH CHOICES

I am a first-generation Mexican American (dual citizen) and the first-born daughter to Mexican immigrants. I have proud and beautiful roots from the border town of Nuevo Laredo, Tamaulipas, Mexico, and the culturally rich town of La Cienega, Zimatlan, Oaxaca, Mexico, all intertwined with being raised in the suburbs of Chicago.

21

My mother was a stay-at-home mom while we were young. Her profession is an early childhood educator, and she went back to it once we grew up. My father was a master mechanic for Ford for thirty-five years before retiring early to run his landscaping business and rental properties full time. I come from humble beginnings, where my frugal mother would shop at Aldi before it was cool and would take us to Jewel at midnight in the summer for the nickel and dime sales. My father worked full-time while side hustling.

If you are the first-born daughter in any Latinx household, you know that we come out of the womb wearing big shoes. We are the "example" for our hermanitos and primos; we are under immense pressure to live correctly and make sure our family knows that their sacrifice of coming to this country was worth it. At a very young age, I saw my parents were very different with our upbringing.

Since I was a little girl, my life consisted of choices. As long as I could remember, my mother always assured us that we had a choice in whatever we did. It started with: "Mija, do you want the Mickey Mouse cup or the Belle cup?" when it was time to eat. My grandmother would be upset and say: "She's a child, just give her one." My mother responded with, "No mami, she needs to know that she always has a choice." Being in my thirties now, I can say that I always knew I had a choice in all I did, and that I should never feel guilty to make the choice for what I want.

My mother taught me at a young age to have self-confidence and to feel comfortable with my choices. My father raised me to never depend on anyone. Ultimately, they raised me to be an interdependent woman, which is such a taboo in the Latinx culture. You see, women raised my father, and he has now become such a feminist and one of my biggest supporters. His words of wisdom always echo in my head. "Mija, eres Chingona, la mas Chingona. Necesitas que terminar tus estudios y comprar tu propia casa, solita. El dia que tu pareja no se porta bien, tu tienes el poder para echarlo a la calle."

So, I did just that, and so much more. When I was eighteen years old, I got out of a short-lived engagement with someone who did not support my dreams and wants. He ultimately cheated on me, and I called the engagement off; and like my papi said, "Lo heches a la calle." A few months later, right before my nineteenth birthday, my mother and I got enough money together so I could purchase a house in cash for $10,000. Now this was during the 2008 recession, and people were losing houses, investments, and businesses left and right. They say that millionaires are created during recessions, and so my mother could have a piece of mind, I bought it for her. Here I was, a community college student, working two retail jobs, and I already had a house paid for since the house was under my name.

I continued on with my studies, and ultimately completed a double master's degrees in business administration and human resources at the age of twenty-eight, all while working full time. In this same year I took my father's other piece of advice: I purchased my own home to live on my own when I chose to move out of my parent's house. Now let me tell you, that process was a challenge within itself. The amount of self-advocacy you do as a Brown woman is outrageous! I always had to reiterate that I was looking for a house that was 100 years old or older, with a yard for my fur baby, and that the mortgage was going to be 25 percent of my take-home salary. I was lucky enough to have a support system behind me. After fifteen rejected offers, and two failed home inspections (I thank the universe for a thorough home inspector), I was about to throw in the towel. But this adorable 118-year-old, small house with beautiful cedar wood floors and a fenced yard came on the market. It was mine! The process was seamless, and I already had a trip to Oaxaca, Mexico, for Día de Los Muertos planned. So, my parents had the honor of being at the closing and my father as my power of attorney. His goal of having "La Mas Chingona" as his daughter came to fruition.

FROM HUMAN RESOURCES PROFESSIONAL TO LATINA BUSINESS OWNER

During my time completing my undergraduate degree, I was lucky enough to get my foot in the door in the human resources field. If you should know anything about HR, it is difficult to get your foot in. I was lucky enough to land an internship with the well-known global company of Bosch. This was when I knew I was different, and that it was a gift to be a bilingual Mexican-American professional. I will never forget when one of the repairmen from the warehouse came up to me during my first week, and the first thing that came out of his mouth was, "You are the only Latina in the front office. Do you understand how big that is? While the workers in the warehouse do not know you yet, we are proud to see one of us making it to a professional position." I held my tears back in front of him but cried on my way home. Here I was a young twenty-four-year-old, and individuals, complete strangers who could be my grandparents, were proud of me. It was as if their own sacrifice of coming to this country had paid off in a way. They got to see the next generation in positions that were their wildest dreams. This was when I realized that my gift should be used to uplift *mi querida raza.*

After the internship ended, I found myself in the manufacturing field, still in the HR profession. That is where I really was able to thrive. I had the mix of American and Latinx culture around me. I could easily relate and cross between both worlds professionally, just as I have personally. During my time with Weber-Stephen Products I was a part of a beautiful HR team, who pushed me to be the best HR professional possible. I was the youngest one on the team, and Anel, Bethy, Gisela, and Miguel took me under their wing right away. This was a space for us to be ourselves, and a safe space for a group of first-generation Mexican Americans who could unapologetically be themselves. For special lunches it was always pollo al carbon instead of sandwiches, or carne asada instead of pizza, and how can I forget, our stash of chiles and hot sauces stashed in our desks. I am forever grateful for that experience, and I have tried creating that same space for my direct reports and team members as I have moved on to other positions. This team is one of the biggest reasons why I was able to finish a double master's in business administration at such a young age. My direct manager, Bethy, let me know after I finished my bachelor of arts degree that if I had a little bit in me to complete a master's to just do it. She promised to support me with tuition reimbursement, schedule, and moral support. She did just that, along with the rest of the team, and in a short two years, at the young age of twenty-eight, I finished graduate school.

After graduation, it was time to take another challenge. I started a position as an HR generalist. I became a part of another team made up of Latinx individuals and was told that this company was going to be a challenge, that there was an opportunity in employee morale. I have always been able to win employees over and create a great working culture, so I took the job. This was in 2019, and less than a year in, the pandemic started. While the pandemic took a toll on a number of professions, HR was one of those that took a huge hit. While I was trying to find my way of working and living in a worldwide pandemic, my mother was also diagnosed with cervical cancer. She was level 1b, which means it was caught early. There were other issues that came up at work, which weren't just about the employee morale. I was becoming more and more miserable there. I wasn't about to leave my job just yet, but I had to make a plan.

During this time, my boyfriend moved in with me so we could go through the global pandemic together, along with my dog, Biscuit, and cat, Luna. This helped slash my bills and mortgage in half, since he took on half of all the bills. People were getting laid off left and right, and I thought I was lucky to even have a job. I started making a plan. I created an emergency fund in a high-yield savings account (HYSA) and hoarded as much money as possible. At this point my living expenses, which included mortgage, utilities, and insurance, were about 14 percent of my salary. I still drove my car from high school because I chose a new car rather than a quinceañera (no car payment!). This meant I could throw a lot into that HYSA. By November 2020, I had saved nine months of living expenses, and I felt comfortable enough to turn in my resignation. That was one of the most liberating things I have ever done in my life, and where the seed was planted for Adriana Talks Dinero, LLC. I remember turning in my resignation and my manager was understanding and asked: "Where will you be going?" I said, "Nowhere. I saved nine months of living expenses, so I can take my time to find a new job." He was shocked and said: "That is a blessing; not all of us can do that." He wished me well. As I spoke to others to let them know I was leaving and told them how I saved enough to take time off, they were all in shock and explained they could never do so. They were in over their heads in debt, and even though they were also unhappy at their positions, they had to work. Mind you, the parking lot was filled with expensive cars/toys, filled with Audis, BMWs, Harley Davidsons, Mercedes, and Lincolns. I was one of the few people with a reserved parking spot who had a car over ten years old. The seed was planted for my small business, but I didn't have the courage or confidence to move on with it.

I ended up at an automotive manufacturing company next, as an HR business partner. This was the job I thought I was going to retire from. I was lucky enough to have a great team and wonderful employees. Once again, I had a great and supportive leader that I reported to. I grew a lot professionally and personally in this chapter of my life. Then, after about nine months, the news was announced we were closing the Elgin, Illinois, facility. All of us were getting laid off. My heart broke and I cried in front of the entire facility as I was translating the president's words. I was happy and content here, and it was all pulled from under me. If you have never been laid off, or been a large component of a layoff, it involves weeks and months of an emotional roller coaster. Here I was, at thirty, getting laid off and laying off over 140 employees along with me. While it was not my decision, I was the one having these hard individual conversations, and I needed to be strong for everyone else. It became a harsh realization that my workforce was not at all ready for a life changing event like losing their job/income. My workforce was over 70 percent Spanish-speaking Latinx individuals, and it opened my eyes to see that they were not at all financially literate and did not know the basics of financial literacy. They made mistakes with money or purchased overpriced homes as we were getting laid off, with no form of income lined up. They had no understanding of their 401(k) and Health Savings Account (HSA), or how unemployment worked in Illinois.

I said to myself: "Something has to give; I need to do something to help out these hardworking people. Use that double MBA for yourself and tu gente, not to make someone else successful." That is when I gained the confidence to start Adriana Talks Dinero. On my thirty-first birthday, I took myself to the Kane County Courthouse to start the process of getting my business name. I got the DBA approved in November. After further research, I saw that a limited liability company (LLC) was the best option for me and my business needs. As I was getting laid off in April, I also was filing my own LLC. As one door closes another one opens.

My mission for Adriana Talks Dinero, LLC *is* to *inspire and empower the minority and disadvantaged with the skills and knowledge to gain a conscious path to financial freedom.* I have seen how disadvantaged the Black, Indigenous, and people of color (BIPOC) community and women are when it comes to finances. As women and immigrants, we put ourselves last. Very few of us plan for the future or have a strong understanding of finances. I remember purchasing my house at twenty-eight and I was not married and needed to have everything in order. I am an avid traveler and never know what the future may hold. I hired an attorney for real estate planning, and she said I am the youngest client she has ever had. No one my age has their living trust, power of attorney or will prepared. The day I get engaged, trust me when I say, the next day I will call my attorney to start on my prenuptial agreement. We have to put ourselves first and protect our wealth.

I have gained a life of peace through being financially stable. I know only a minority of the American population feels the same. A recent study has found that "90 percent of Americans say that money impacts their stress level."1 I want everyone to feel the same liberation when they are able to quit a toxic job, leave their cheating partner, or feel secure when they find out they are getting laid off. Adriana Talks Dinero, LLC is changing people's way of thinking about money, and it will change people's lives in the process. This is the legacy I am leaving behind for future generations and my gift to the world.

MY FINANCE INSPIRATION

Finance actually chose me in a sense. I was originally in human resources, but I saw my gift and education could be better served in financial literacy education and money coaching. I had a professor in my graduate program for finance and accounting who taught us the subjects in a way that we could fully understand. His goal was to teach us how to retire one day and how not to get scammed by brokerage managers, to ultimately do it ourselves.

Finance is incredibly important; we live in a capitalistic society. Without money we wouldn't be able to survive. It is up to us as Latinas to be the best we can in our personal finances and the finance field, and to share the wealth of knowledge with as many people as possible.

Questions for Readers

1. Were you ever at a job you were not happy at for too long? Why?
2. Imagine you had financial freedom, what would that look and feel like?

3. If you pass away tomorrow, would your family be financially and legally prepared for this life changing event?

Cited Work

1. White, Alexandria. "90% Of Americans Say Money Impacts Their Stress Level, According to New 'Thriving Wallet' Study by Thrive Global and Discover." CNBC, CNBC, 29 August 2022, https://www.cnbc.com/select/why-americans-are-stressed-about-money/#:~:text=90%25%20of%20Americans%20Stress%20About%20Money%2C%20According%20to%20Study%20Results.

BIOGRAPHY

Adriana Galvan is a Mexican American (dual citizen) born and raised in Elgin, Illinois. She is the first-born daughter of immigrant parents. Her father is from La Cienega, Zimatlan, Oaxaca, Mexico, and her mother is from Nuevo Laredo, Tamaulipas, Mexico.

Education was instilled in her life at a young age. Which helped her have a successful educational career at a young age. She graduated from Elgin Community College in 2013 with an associates of arts degree. In 2016, she graduated from Judson University with a bachelor of arts degree. Adriana finished her double master's in business administration in 2019 from The Graham School of Management at Saint Xavier University.

One of Adriana's passions is traveling. She is well known for traveling to foreign countries, even alone, without any fears. She also never forgets where she comes from, being the only grandchild from both sides of the family who makes yearly trips to Mexico to visit family. Another of her passions is people, and she is deeply involved with a number of organizations that help her community thrive, such as The Elgin Hispanic Network, Latinas on the Plaza, The Literacy Connection, and Rise and Thrive Latinas.

She started her career in human resources and has taken the opportunity to be a Latina business owner with her financial literacy education and money coaching business. She is the owner and founder of Adriana Talks Dinero, LLC. She wants to inspire and empower the minority and disadvantaged with the skills and knowledge to gain a conscious path to financial freedom with her small business.

Adriana Galvan, MBA
(224) 689-4525
www.adrianatalksdinero.com
info@adrianatalksdinero.com
Facebook: @adrianatalksdinero
Instagram: @adrianatalksdinero
Twitter: @adrianatalksdinero
TikTok: @adrianatalksdinero

MICHELLE J. VELASQUEZ

———

"Financial education starts at home! Teach your children about what money means to you and what you value about money."

THE WAKEUP CALL

It was around 2 a.m. when the phone rang. I immediately knew something bad had happened. I could hear my sister Veronica crying, attempting to tell me it was about dad. As I hurried into the hospital, I saw a priest standing next to my mother. That day forever changed my life. My hero, my cheerleader, my protector, my provider, and my best friend had been taken away so unexpectedly. This tragic loss was the beginning of my financial journey.

SHATTERED DREAM

As my sisters and I planned our dad's funeral, I saw all the expenses adding up. For the past twenty-eight years, my father had paid for almost everything in my life. Prior to my father's death, I thought I was living "my dream." However, as I started to look at my bank accounts, I realized that I literally had no money to my name. I did what most desperate people do in an emergency—take out a loan on my retirement account. This was the ONLY way I could contribute to help pay for my dad's funeral. Reviewing my accounts carefully made me realize how much debt I had accumulated over the years. The only place I had money saved was in the one account that I knew I should NEVER withdraw from, my retirement account. I vividly remember crying in my room, thinking how I never wanted anyone else to feel the way I did. I felt so helpless. I couldn't believe that I didn't have enough money saved to help bury the most important man in my life—my loving father. How does this "college graduate with a master's degree" and a "good job" not have a savings? After all, I was supposed to have a better education and better opportunities than my parents. At least, that's the mentality most people in my family had. In that moment, I was stuck in the earn-and-spend cycle. In this cycle, we earn money but spend all of it with no real intention. We work hard for our money; however, sadly we have no idea where it actually goes. We spend money on things we don't value.

A few weeks after my dad's passing, I began to declutter and organize his office. On his desk was a green book on financial freedom. When I saw that book, still wrapped, it sparked my interest. Why did dad need this book? That was my "AHA!" moment and a turning point in my life. In that pivotal moment, I realized that my father's heart attack was due to his financial stress. I removed the wrapper and opened it. I had to seize the opportunity that my father no longer had, which was to read the book. I became fascinated and addicted to reading and learning about money management.

THE SIGNIFICANCE OF A WILL

It felt like the world was on my shoulders. I was now responsible for reading my father's mind. My father died at the age of fifty-seven from an unexpected heart attack. He died WITHOUT a will. I spent countless hours in his office trying to put together the pieces to this puzzle. After twelve years, I can tell you, I never did. I tried really hard to put myself in his place and read his post-it notes, ledgers, journals, notebooks, receipts, etc. I learned that having a will would have saved me so much time and money. When you die without a will, it leaves your family in the dark with no plan and feeling frustrated. They are unaware of your wishes. Lack of a will, in many instances causes conflict within families, especially when it comes to deciding what happens to your assets.

THE IMPORTANCE OF FINANCIAL CLARITY

When my father passed away, I was the only daughter not married. Culturally, I was expected to move in and take care of my mom, which I did. I was now responsible for managing her financial affairs. Dad was a loving father and a provider with a generous, giving heart. As the man of the household, he handled all the financial matters just like in most traditional Mexican homes. My mom was responsible for always having a warm cooked meal. Let me tell you, NO WOMAN could ever beat her cooking skills. During my first sit down with my mother regarding dad's estate, I realized she knew NOTHING about the bills, mortgages, credit cards, bank accounts, business, etc. Dad believed the less she knew the better. In his mind, he was doing mom a favor by simply taking care of everything. Financial dependency leaves women feeling lost and insecure of their future when their husband dies. When women survive their spouses, normally they will inherit money or assets and have no idea what to do with that money. When you get no guidance, the money soon gets exhausted. As a financial coach, I provide women with financial clarity. Having financial clarity is so important; it helps you to understand where you are financially and where you want to be in the future. Having financial clarity is imperative because it allows you to plan for yourself and your children's future.

LATINO HOUSEHOLDS

Like many Latino households, money was not a conversation we had at the dinner table. We didn't grow up listening to our parents talk about their savings, budgets, retirement accounts, or investments. Instead, we grew up in a home where parents always prioritized education. They knew that if we would obtain a college degree, we would have a higher standard of living and "do better" than them. The goal of Latino parents is for their children to "struggle less" than they did. My parents wanted us to use "our brains and not our physical backs." We heard things like "estudien para que no se maten el lomo." In my home, college wasn't an option but a requirement. The only option we had was which college we were going to attend. As a Latina, I grew up listening to my parents' advice—we better study hard and go to college so we can graduate and get a "good" job. And when we got these jobs, we were reminded that we should be grateful that we have a job. Even today, my mother constantly tells me: "Mija dale gracias a Dios que tienes trabajo."

EDUCATION AND ENTREPRENEURSHIP

What many parents are actually doing is encouraging their children to go to school, graduate, and get a job working for SOMEONE ELSE. Instead, we need to challenge our children and motivate them to become entrepreneurs. Being an entrepreneur is viewed as taking a big risk. My father was a risk taker and he encouraged us to take risks. He believed that we should start our own business versus making someone else rich.

MY DEBT-FREE JOURNEY

After college, I started a career in law enforcement. However, my desire to learn about money grew more and more. There was an increase in officer suicides within the law enforcement community and my agency decided to offer a financial program for employees and their families as a preventive approach. My husband and I elected to participate in the financial program. I had $88,000 in consumer and student debt, so this was exactly what we needed! Following the program, I was determined to start our debt-free journey. Like many couples at that time, we had separate finances, but we felt God asking us to trust each other and merge our finances as we were one under God. We worked hard with one goal, and that was to change our family tree by redirecting our financial trajectory. As Christians, we believe that "a good man leaves an inheritance to his children's children" (Proverbs 13:22). This was the turning point in my financial journey, where I decided that we were going to let our money work for us instead of working for money.

Being free of $88,000 dollars in debt was a dream come true! Getting rid of debt allowed me to use my income to work for me. Society makes us feel like it is normal to be in debt as everyone else is, too. The reality is that you shouldn't be worried about everyone else's finances but your own. Personal finance is exactly that PERSONAL.

THE BIRTH OF VIRTUOUS WEALTH BUILDING

One night at about 3 a.m., I woke up and was led by the Holy Spirit to open my bible. The Holy Spirit led me to Proverbs 31—where it talks about the virtuous woman. In Proverbs 31, the bible defines a virtuous woman as one who leads her home with integrity and discipline. The bible tells us that a virtuous woman is clothed with strength and dignity. It also tells us that a virtuous woman watches over the affairs of her household. All the virtues she strives for are to make her husband's life better, teaching her children, and serving God. This was now the beginning to my God-given assignment.

MINDSET

As I began to coach, I was inspired by the impact my coaching was having in the lives of countless women. One of the common challenges that women face when it comes to money is…mindset. I've often encountered women who believe, "I am bad with money," but they realize that they can learn how to manage their money. On many occasions, women will believe, "I cannot afford this." They learn to shift their mind and now say, what can I do to be able to afford this?" I often encourage women to know what they value about money, and once they have identified what it is they value, this will allow them to stay focused on their financial goals. Knowing what you value about money will allow you to make better financial decisions for your future.

CLARITY

Some of the common money struggles I've helped Latina moms deal with are not having clarity of where their money is going, feeling stressed and frustrated about their financial situation, having separate finances with spouses, marital stress over money, student loan debt, overspending, not knowing how to save and budget, knowledge of retirement accounts, and stressed moms not knowing how will they help pay for college for their children.

COACHING

As a coach, I have successfully helped women pay off credit card debt which ranged from $5,000 to $46,000. I've also witness women selling their current homes and upgrading homes. Other women began saving for the down payments of their future investment properties. I've created personalized debt strategies to pay off student loan debts. On one occasion, I helped a widow obtain $50,000 in survivor benefits for her teenage daughter after fifteen years of her husband's death. It has been inspiring to coach and walk step by step along the journey of these women and couples.

TEACHING OUR CHILDREN

Financial education starts at home. Teach your children about what money means to you, and what you value about money. Make them feel like they are part of the daily financial decisions, and, most importantly, teach them to partner with God. As parents, we are responsible for encouraging our children. At the age of eight, my son, Marty, launched his snow cone business. As parents, we should motivate our children to become entrepreneurs, so they can have flexibility and freedom when they become adults. At the age of six, Izan was able to get his first bank debit card. He is currently learning about saving and spending. Even my little ones, Joe and Adaleah, both have their piggy banks. Teach your children to take care of what they have, so they can learn to value what they have.

THE SECRET

As a coach to Latina moms, I found a common secret they share. The majority of these moms experience guilt. These moms desperately cry inside, wanting to be financially free so they can be able to spend more time with their children. These moms experience an internal struggle with the idea of being a working mom and the choice to spend more time with their children. They desire flexibility and freedom to choose to stay home and raise their children. On the one hand, they are supposed to "be better" than their mothers, yet at the same time, their children "need them." My mission as founder of Virtuous Wealth Building is to help Latina moms discover their God-given talents and teach them to manage their money, so they can have the freedom they desire.

My father used to tell me, "No one can take your education away." I leave you with my father's advice, which is to continue to invest in yourselves daily, whether it's listening to a podcast, reading a book, reading the newspaper, investing in a workshop, or joining my coaching program. You hold the power of your daily choices. Your motivation, "Your WHY," needs to be strong and always present.

MY FINANCE INSPIRATION

Women are the heart of the family, and we have tremendous power to change the trajectory of our family's financial future. Learn to partner with God as He desires to overflow you with his abundance.

BIOGRAPHY

Michelle J. Velasquez is the founder and CEO of Virtuous Wealth Building. She is a financial coach who is passionate about educating, encouraging, and empowering, Latina moms to take control of their finances and build generational wealth while partnering up with God.

Michelle is happily married to her husband, Martin Arteaga. They have been blessed with four beautiful children: Marty (nine), Izan (seven), Joe (five) and Adaleah (two). Michelle is the daughter of (the late) Joe J. Velasquez and Ofelia Velasquez. Michelle has four sisters: Edith, Cristina, Yajaira, and Veronica.

For the past fifteen years, Michelle has served as a federal law enforcement officer with the U.S. Department of Homeland Security. She is also a real estate investor with her husband and creating wealth through Airbnbs, flipping homes, and real estate coaching via Green Building Partners, Inc.

Michelle received her bachelor and master degrees from Loyola University Chicago. In addition, she is a proud sister of Gamma Phi Omega International Sorority, Inc.

Michelle is a member of New Life Community Church. During a business conference, Michelle felt a strong calling to become a financial coach. She knows God created her to be a woman of impact and purpose. She truly enjoys sharing her testimony with you.

Michelle J. Velasquez

Financial coach

Virtuous Wealth Building

www.vwbcoaching.com

info@vwbcoaching.com

Facebook and Instagram: @vwbcoaching

Motto: "Be blessed, not stressed."

INSISTING, PERSISTING, AND RESISTING!

JACKIE CARPINTERO

"We should live and work passionately and value every moment. The most important part of a business is not just making money. The most important thing is the contribution and help given to each person. Let's keep doing our best to help other people fulfill their dreams!"

In this part of my story, you will come across an exciting journey! By the end of the chapter, my dearest readers, you will conclude whether my path has been easy or complicated.

On October 2, 1987, I experienced one of the most difficult goodbyes of my life. I was a heartbroken teenager at El Dorado Airport in Bogotá, Colombia, as I said goodbye to my boyfriend and hugged my mother and my relatives without knowing when I would see them again. I will never forget the words of the strong and brave woman who always did whatever it took to get my brothers and I ahead in life. She said: "Everything will be fine. When we're done with our goodbyes, don't look back. Look towards your future. Great opportunities are waiting for you, I'm sure of it." I listened, and after time had passed, my mother told me that this had been one of the saddest days of her life.

I spent eight days traveling through Mexico City alongside my brother, Jorge, where we experienced lots of different situations, some scary, some funny and some very unpleasant, but together we fought every day to achieve our goal of crossing the border to reach the United States. Fortunately, on November 2, 1987, we managed to set foot on American soil and meet up with our uncle on our mother's side, Jairo, who was anxiously waiting for us after eight long days with no communication.

In January 1988, I got my first job at the Hotel Holiday Inn in Itasca, Illinois, where I cleaned rooms for $4.00 an hour. The challenge was that I had to clean sixteen rooms in eight hours with no experience, not enough time, and no idea how to do it. But I found the solution. When I would start running out of time, I would offer my coworkers $3.00 an hour to help me finish the job. It was my first work experience and I quickly realized that this was not the kind of job I wanted for my life.

After two months, I got a better job at a gaming machine production factory earning $4.50 an hour. I was progressing, but it was clear to me that I was not fit for those kinds of jobs. During this time, I married the father of my children, but I was still unsatisfied with my career. I knew that I would not progress any further if I did not try harder. So, after two years of living in Chicago, I decided to return to Colombia to finish my degree in business administration. These were unforgettable years in school where I met wonderful people, among them were people who are still my best friends today. I graduated and returned to the U.S. with the vision of being an administrator.

I then got a job at an employment company as a telemarketer. My goal was to become the manager of that office. So, I would finish my work quickly to assist the current manager and learn what her duties were. Fortunately, at the time, she was pregnant, and when it came time for her maternity leave, I was immediately chosen to fill the vacancy in her position. Pretty soon I became the administrator for not only my office, but six other ones in the company. By then, I was already earning $18.00 an hour, which was a good salary back then. I had gotten more than what I had imagined, but at the expense of having no life because the stress overwhelmed me.

One day, one of my colleagues invited me to a life insurance meeting. I remembered that when I was only ten years old, several months before my father died, a life insurance agent explained to him the importance of having insurance, and fortunately, he accepted the offer. I am incredibly grateful for that man who practically saved my family. My father had made one of the best decisions of his life because my family did not struggle with financial problems when he passed away, and I cannot imagine what would have happened to my family if we had not had that insurance. Looking back at that, I thought, *I can be one of those heroes and help save families from misfortune*. It was at that moment that I realized that my vocation was to contribute towards the wellbeing of others. So, I accepted the job opportunity but continued working in my current role at the time. After work in the afternoons, I would study with great enthusiasm knowing that I had found what I was looking for. One of the first challenges I faced was the language barrier. The textbook was in English, but a dictionary solved that problem, as well as my mother's motto which was always in the back of my head: "You can do it."

Starting out was not easy because I did not have an extensive client portfolio. But I had already promised myself that I would become my own boss and not be a slave to an employee work schedule. This time, my goal was to become independent no matter what. I would fearlessly strike up a conversation with people I met and offer them my service daily. There were many days that I would work long hours prospecting but would come home with no sales. I felt sad and regretted that I was not going to be able to do it, but I would hear the phrase, "You came to this country to succeed. You can do it." Do you know who it was? My mother, who had moved in with us. She was my biggest supporter and motivator. When she arrived, my beloved son, Michael, was seven months old; she was a blessing in our lives.

Every time I heard that phrase from my mother it filled me with energy to keep going and I did it with more enthusiasm. And just like that, she was right! I was doing it! I began to build my portfolio of clients, which led to more business. One day I was closing an insurance deal with a client when he asked if I could help him refinance his house. Immediately, my answer was, "Yes, of course!" On the way back home, I was thinking that if I studied to get a loan officer license, I could combine the two businesses. I went home, excited to tell my beloved mentor, and what do you think she said?

"You can do it." Without thinking twice about it, I searched for a broker and got to work the very next day. I signed up for morning classes and took care of my life insurance clients in the afternoons. Let me tell you, getting that license is not easy. I failed the first time I took the exam, but I already had a client waiting for me. I studied fiercely day after day until I passed. I was now a life insurance agent and a loan officer. I was happily able to assist my client and continued forward.

I set out to learn every detail from A to Z about this business, while pregnant with my princess, Natalie. My then-husband and I, decided to partner with one of my insurance associates to open a mortgage office called SC Financial Services, LLC. We represent banks and generate job opportunities for new representatives and people who want to start out in the industry. We were able to help many clients obtain a loan to buy a home. After a while, the clients would even ask us to be their representatives in the purchase of the property, my answer always being, "Yes, of course!"

New challenge: Study to get a real estate license. This license was even more difficult to get than the last one! When the idea popped into my head, immediately I could hear my mom saying the words in my head: "You can do it." Sure enough, a couple of months later, the father of my children and I became real estate agents. We partnered with REMAX to do that sort of business.

We began to invest in houses that were in poor condition. We would then remodel and sell them. It was years of hard work, but very productive ones, and we managed to reach financial stability.

My mother applauded us every day and spoiled us with her delicious meals. She was happy to know how much we had already achieved. She was a fundamental part of our professional growth and was a blessing to our lives.

Unfortunately, on February 4, 2004, when my son Michael had just turned eight years old, and my daughter Natalie, four years old, I experienced the most painful day of my life. My mother passed away from a cardiovascular aneurysm. It was devastating for everyone; just remembering brings tears to my eyes. I felt a deep emptiness, so strong that at times I thought I was not going to be able to move forward in my life. In those moments when I was filled with sadness, I would hear her voice: "You can do it." I do not know how, but that was one of the most productive years we had. Business was booming.

In 2007, we made the worst mistake of our lives. A good friend told me that the Trump Tower was being built in Chicago, and that it would be a promising investment. So, I convinced the father of my children, as well as our partner, to consider the project. We saw it and found it interesting. The plan was to buy it at its low price while under construction and then immediately sell it when it was finished, at a higher price to make a profit. The price of a one-bedroom apartment was $1 million. We paid $300,000 as a down payment. We were going to ask for a loan from the bank for the remaining $700,000.

One day, in 2008, we woke up to the news about the country's economy collapsing. Not only did we lose our jobs, but we lost the $300,000 because the banks were no longer offering the loan we needed. Everything collapsed on us. From one day to the next, we lost twenty years' worth of work. The worst thing was the fact that we still had the responsibility to continue paying the mortgage for the other houses we owned. Our lives turned upside down.

Petrified, we wondered what we were going to do. We had made a big mistake! We had put all our eggs in the same basket; all our investments were in real estate, and it was the most affected industry at the time. These were dark and weary days.

A few weeks later, I received a call from one of my clients whom I had helped get a loan for her house. She said she had lost her job and had no way of paying for her mortgage. She asked if I could help, and my answer was, "Yes, of course!" At that moment I thought, *I have experience working with banks and surely many people will be going through the same problem. They will not be able to pay their home loans and the banks will have to do something.* So, I immediately called my accountant; we registered a company called American Loan Modification, LLC. We knew this business would be temporary, but it was a rewarding thing we were doing, helping many families save their homes from foreclosure. It was one of the most difficult experiences of my career, but it helped me to grow personally and professionally. One of the skills I developed the most was solving problems quickly and reinventing myself. During that time as well, I took a course on tax preparation, and to this day I still help some of my clients in that area.

In November 2016, I committed myself one hundred percent to the area of life insurance, and in 2017, Chicago Financial Group (CFG), LLC was registered.

Today, CFG is a financial services agency that represents a wide range of life insurance and annuity companies with the best ratings in the industry, which have been insuring millions of families for decades. CFG's focus is to help protect family assets with something as essential as life insurance. We are operating with a new concept of life insurance which says: "That you do not have to die to use your insured amount." In the case of a critical, chronic, or terminal illness, the insured can receive a percentage of their benefits while they are alive to use towards medical expenses and continue their quality of life. Similarly, the program has a savings vehicle that earns quite attractive interest rates. Best of all, those savings are tax free.

Does your life insurance have all these benefits?

MY FINANCE INSPIRATION

I chose finance because of the firsthand experiences I had because of my father's death. My family was able to move forward because of the benefits of having life insurance. It inspired me to help the Latino community and to be one of those heroes who show families that life insurance is the financial foundation of a home. You may wonder why, and the reason is that if a family survives with X amount of monthly income and one of the providers becomes ill or dies, where will that income come from now?

Today, no matter what career you have or are about to embark on, finance is defined as the art and science of managing money, something that plays a role in the lives of every single person, family, and organization. Studying finance can prepare you not only for careers in the financial service sector, but also for daily life. Finance revolves around planning and analysis, so embarking on a career in this field and becoming more financially literate enables people to make better personal financial decisions.

I have had the opportunity to participate in several seminars, including one in which Robert T. Kiyosaki came to Chicago to promote his book, which he wrote in collaboration with Donald J. Trump, titled *Why We Want You to Be Rich*. There is a quote in the book that says: "Money problems are not solved with money; they are solved with knowledge." Daily preparation is a fundamental part of any professional career!

BIOGRAPHY

Entrepreneurial, passionate, ambitious, enthusiastic, yet humble by nature, Jackie was born and raised in Bogota, Colombia, and holds a degree in business administration. Jackie relocated to Chicago in 1987, in search of better opportunities. Jackie quickly found her passion helping people achieve their financial dreams. Over the years, she has worked in different branches of the industry, starting as a life insurance agent and later becoming a loan officer, real estate broker, and tax preparer.

After the economic crash in 2008, Jackie founded American Loan Modification, LLC and, in collaboration with various banks, was able to help many of her clients get out of foreclosure and stay in their homes.

Today, Jackie draws on her vast experience in finance as CEO and founder of Chicago Financial Group (CFG), LLC since 2017. CFG is an agency that represents various high-quality life insurance companies in the industry, providing a wide range of financial services that help the community protect their assets and fulfill their dreams.

Over the last few years, Jackie has dedicated herself to expanding CFG to other states, recruiting and training other professionals to become the leading company that trains life insurance agents, and whose main goal is to educate and help the public make the best financial decisions for their future.

Jackie and her group of professionals have managed to meetproduction and reputation expectations with each company she represents. Jackie and her team have insured thousands of families and have managed to work honorably and impeccably within the industry!

Jackie Carpintero
chicagofinancial13@gmail.com
(630) 863-8324 and (847) 466-7162
https://www.cfgagency.com

WITH FAITH, ANYTHING IS POSSIBLE

GLENDA ALVARADO

"This continues to be a country of opportunities, and the world of finance offers us, Hispanics, that chance."

Faith is not an easy subject to discuss given what it is: certainty for what is to come and conviction of what you do not see.

The faith to provide a better future for my children, my three-year-old twin boys, is what pushed me to make the hard decision to leave my home, my native land, the city of Guayaquil, Ecuador. I left everything behind, burned my bridges, and did not take anything material with me that would make me want to go back. I threw myself into an uncertain future as I traveled without any knowledge of the English language, but with only a tourist visa and faith that I would find my way regardless of the pain of leaving behind my family, including my parents, siblings, grandparents, uncles, aunts, and lifelong friends. I was a twenty-eight-year-old woman determined to carry my children and my marriage forward. My children's father had traveled to the United States beforehand, and the plan was to meet again in a foreign country that would offer us the opportunities that our own country could not. At the time we decided to leave, Ecuador was going through a recession, which forced us to close our business distributing automotive paint. I would never want to be away from my children, I could not endure living far from them. I thank God that my parents have always supported me. My father traveled with me when I left to help me with the kids. He has always been my guardian angel, my role model and guide. Now, he lives in Ecuador with my mother, and they are my full responsibility, which I consider a blessing given that they are alive and well. That is my drive, which remains strong, to never stop fighting for the wellbeing of my own.

Having faith has taken me to places I would have never been able to reach without confidently knowing that I am not alone. The internal strength that I get from believing in God is what has allowed me to reach not one, but all the goals that I have wanted to achieve.

Adversity and difficult situations are much more manageable when we are aware that everything that is outside of our control we can leave in God's hands. We do our part, and He oversees everything else. I was given the opportunity to enter the world of mortgages in 1998, a time when Bill Clinton was president and the FHA program interests were at 8.5 percent. I started as a part-time telemarketer at a mortgage company (that no longer exists). I used to make appointments for lenders to offer their mortgage refinancing services, and I would say to myself, "This isn't so complicated," because I was good at quoting people. I had finance knowledge coming in as I had worked in the operating staff at a bank back in my native country, as well as graduated from the Laica University Vicente Rocafuerte of Guayaquil in administrative science. Although I did not know much English, I thought, numbers are numbers and I know that I can do this. Self-confidence is important to be able to achieve the goals we set for ourselves. However, there is always someone who instead of motivating you, will say, "How do you expect to work with mortgages? You have no legal rights in this country." My tourist visa expired, and I did not know enough English to get by, but my desire to move forward went beyond any obstacle or person that instilled insecurity instead of supporting me. That was how God opened doors. I found a place that trained me; and the rest is history. I am always grateful for God and for the people who gave me the opportunity to start out in the wonderful world of mortgages. I became the manager of an agency (that is no longer in the market), and I also had my own marketing company, where I offered advertising packages for homeowners who wanted to sell their homes without a real estate agent, getting them direct sales and, thus, saving money on commissions, since house values had gone up exponentially. Offering them advertising packages allowed them to do this on their own.

Shortly after that the mortgage market collapsed, leading many companies to close their doors in 2008, I found myself completely lost, not knowing where to turn. The programs that had been offered were no longer in the market. This meant that many could not refinance their homes because the programs offered at that time had two types of loans, homebuyer's incomes did not have to qualify to buy a home, but by removing the programs it was impossible for people to refinance their homes and not lose them due to the disproportionate increase in their mortgage payments. So, things got complicated for me career-wise, personally, and economically. It is incredible how sometimes people will hold on to a relationship for convenience when they are going through difficult situations. I also had made the decision to separate myself from the father of my children. My residency status was at risk when I decided to do this, but that did not stop me from ending an unsalvageable relationship. If I would have had Christ in my heart back then the way I do now, perhaps I would have wanted to try to work things out. At that time, I decided to face life on my own. I was criticized. But in the end, I learned how to make decisions without considering the opinions of those who do not matter and who do not contribute in any way to my life. At the end of the day, it was my life, they were my children, and I got to decide what I considered was the best for me and for them at that moment.

It was in this period that I decided to get a life insurance license to offer financial plans that included term insurance and the possibility of saving money in annuities, as well as mutual funds for people to start building their assets. These also would allow them to prepare in case of a premature death so as not to leave their families unprotected.

A funeral is the second most costly expense that families have, after buying a car. They range between $6,000 and $20,000. In other words, even dying is expensive, and generally speaking, the Hispanic community is not very well known for having the habit of saving up and preparing for any eventuality. So, I stayed in finance, but this time, in the field of life insurance, savings, and investment, to help families stay prepared in these areas. I am passionate about everything that has to do with numbers. I enjoy programming events to get the Hispanic community more involved and educated so that the newer generations find themselves better off. Hispanic people are not just found in the labor force. Our children have the option to follow career paths in finance, politics, economics, and science, making an actual difference in this country, and without letting others make decisions for us.

In 2012, I met the man who became my second husband, Ivan Fabre, another Guayaquileño.

Life and God wanted us to meet here in Chicago in an Ecuadorian restaurant, where he would go to eat, and I would go to look for potential clients for my financial programs. Just like that, we started our relationship. He procured a financial plan for himself, which first led to a friendship being born and then love that lasted ten years. Unfortunately, my husband lost his life on January 9, 2022, due to COVID-19, another victim of the pandemic.

My husband was like an angel of light in my life. Not only did he love me, but he was always someone who believed in me and motivated me to be and give the best. He was an amazing life partner, he encouraged me to get my mortgage loan originator license again. I thank God, because without his support I could not have achieved this. With my faith placed in God, and with significant effort, I managed to get my loan license once more by the end of 2018; something that has been extremely rewarding is achieving my goals. Getting back into the mortgage business has given me the wonderful opportunity to once again network with people who yearn to be homeowners, and when they come to me and I get to help them in this process, it brings great satisfaction to fulfill my duties. Every client is a challenge for me. Many come with complicated circumstances, which no one has been able to assist them with. When they come and I tell them they do qualify, they are shocked. I always tell my clients: "I am not just a collector of documents; I am a qualified and experienced professional that intends to connect you with a program that suits your circumstances." Currently, in the mortgage market, there is wide variety of mortgage loans that can be adjusted to the needs of a person, whether you are a first-time homeowner, investor, business owner, or even someone who does not yet have legal status in this country. Programs already exist that allow us to serve immigrants who, as previously mentioned, do not yet have a legal status in this country. This continues to be a country of opportunities, and the world of finance offers us, Hispanics, that chance. I currently offer seminars, taught entirely in Spanish, to continue educating and preparing Hispanic families who are on the path to achieving the American dream and purchasing their homes.

The world of finance will always offer us opportunities and options; our decisions are what matter. In life, we will always come across difficult situations that may bring tears to our eyes and push us to a breaking point, but it is at that moment when faith begins to act. We must trust in the one who never abandons us, the one who allows us to move forward, the one who gives us strength when we do not have any, who perfects us in our weakness, and helps us reach the unimaginable. Let love always be that great and powerful reason that pushes you to reach places that you never thought you could reach. Let the perseverance to achieve your dreams always keep you steady and smiling. Stay thankful, because even in our days of darkness, God always gives us a reason to smile and keep living. I say that as someone who lost their life partner. I honor his memory and our love through this story. If there was anything of his that stuck with me after the fact, it was his joy, his desire to live and enjoy life, and his faith in Jesus, our beloved Savior. With Him, everything is possible. I hope that my story inspires you to achieve your goals. With love, faith, and hard work, anything is possible. Therefore, I hope that there are many Latina women who feel strong and capable of achieving their hopes and dreams. Remember, we are not alone. God is always with us, and if God is for me, who can be against me?

MY FINANCE INSPIRATION

What motivated me to get involved in the world of finance was my interest in it from an early age. As a child, I always wanted to work in a banking institution. When I came to the United States, I did not stop myself from searching for the first opportunity to do this. To be able to offer my children a better future has always been my inspiration, and my late husband, Ivan Fabre, was the engine that supported me, and to whom I dedicate this book. His dedication, his love, and all the support he gave me has motivated me to get my loan originator license again. He would always tell me that I had to be independent despite having him as my husband. He wanted me to be a woman who could have the world at her fingertips, as I had been before. With his love, he helped me overcome my fears and insecurities, and now that he is gone, I continue to enjoy the fulfilling life that he helped me build. If it were not for God, and for loving what I do for a living, I would not be standing today. Today, I thank God for having given me a life partner who played an instrumental role in my getting back into the wonderful world of mortgages. I know that he looks down proudly on me and says: "My Glendita is a woman full of faith, a strong woman."

"I can do all things through Christ who strengthens me."
Philippians 4:13

BIOGRAPHY

Glenda Alvarado was born in Guayaquil, Ecuador, on January 24, 1969, to Gloria Yance and Luis Alvarado, the first-born daughter of three children, the other two being boys. Glenda went to primary school at Escuela Particular La Providencia, and high school at the Providencia Private School, then graduated in administrative sciences from the Vicente Rocafuerte Lay University of Guayaquil. She was an assistant for the management of a banking agency, Banco de Prestamos, in Guayaquil, Ecuador, from 1990 to 1992. Glenda was also the owner of an automotive painting business from 1992 to 1996, manager of the office of First Financial Mortgage in 2002, and owner of Solo by Owner Advertising Agency from 2006 to 2008.

Currently, Glenda is a licensed life insurance agent, a licensed mortgage agent, and a member of the National Association of Hispanic Real Estate Professionals. She is dedicated to helping families obtain adequate financing for the purchase of their homes with programs that range from zero percent down payment to programs for Individual Taxpayer Identification Number (ITIN) individuals and Deferred Action for Childhood Arrivals (DACA). She is a member of the New Vision Community Church Casa de Oración, where she collaborates in event planning and programming in Cicero, Illinois. In her free time, she organizes community food pantries, informative workshops, and other church activities to help and serve the needy while sharing the gospel and helping Hispanic families. Glenda always looks for a way to serve others because "he who does not live to serve, is not good at living."

Glenda Alvarado

glendaloans@yahoo.com

Facebook: @GlendaAlvarado

THE TREE OF ABUNDANCE

MARIA RAMOS-CUAYA

"Talking about finances is a very personal conversation, and I encourage you to never compare your story to anyone else's."

I was born and raised in the colorful state of Puebla, Mexico, land of the Olmec, Toltec, Mixtec, Popoloca, Totonac, Mazatec and Otomi. I am the granddaughter of Cruz Cuaya and Angela Castillo Yanez and daughter of Maria del Carmen Cuaya Castillo. My mother migrated to California to work as a farm worker; and after almost a decade of working in the fields, she moved and settled in Chicago, Illinois, land of the Potawatomi Winnebago/Ho-Chunk, Otoe, Missouria, Iowas, Menominee, Meskwaki, Sauk, Miami, Wea, Piankashaw, Kickapoo, Inoka, Ojibwe and Odawa. I joined my mother at the age of twelve and have called Chicago my second home since.

As a child I always knew in my heart that as an adult I would be driven by love and passion. I have felt that immense energy my whole life. I got my master's degree in urban planning and public policy because I loved the vision of contributing to creating healthy and strong communities. In a healthy community, all residents should have access to affordable housing, education, employment, transportation, spaces for physical activities, quality healthcare and opportunities for economic development, to name a few. Unfortunately, a history of redlining, segregation and discrimination has made it very hard for our communities of color to have access to the financial benefits of homeownership and community development. Housing policies in the history of this country have created systemic racial barriers and biases. In the last decade I have intentionally focused my professional career in closing the racial wealth gap by working for organizations that are committed to advocating for new public housing policies, to provide housing counseling services and access to financial services and homeownership. I have had the honor to lead a team of passionate and committed housing counselors that provided pre-purchase, post-purchase and homeless prevention counseling. I have worked among leaders and colleagues dedicated to community development outreach and engagement, and I have served as a financial coach and financial educator. During the pandemic I was able to assist families to access financial assistance in migrant communities of color, which are still facing the socioeconomic costs of COVID-19. The journey has been full of wins, and lessons learned, and it has shaped me into the leader I am today.

One of the best lessons learned has been my own financial wellness journey. So, where do we begin? I'll begin by answering the question I ask my clients in my financial wellness workshops: What is your first memory of money?

As a young child, I remember doing chores with my grandma and making sure that I always listened to her and did all my homework. Little Maria knew that when Sunday came around, my grandpa would give me "mi domingo," a few pesos for being good, so I could save it to get a snack at the grocery store. It was so exciting to get to go to the store and look at the rack full of crunchy flavorful chips and the counter with a variety of chocolates and colorful Mexican candy. Then there was the rack of pastry sweets! I couldn't say no to a gansito or a pack of galletas Marias. I had a big decision to make because I didn't have enough pesos for more than one item, but it was still such a fun experience.

I also have very vivid memories of going to the mercado with my grandmother and aunts, I loved those times. The mercado was huge. I remember thinking, how does one not get lost in this labyrinth? My grandmother used to hold on so tight to my wrist that it hurt, but I enjoyed my stroll between mountains of apples, mangos, jicamas, limes, lemons, chiles, oranges, guanabanas, guavas, nopales, cilantro, and aguacates. Somehow, I knew my grandmother had enough money to buy what we needed, because we always had food on the table. My reasoning was that my grandfather and my mom were away so much, working very hard to take care of us.

When we were done shopping and left the mercado, there were small children, younger than little Maria, begging for money. Some were selling handmade crafts or nuts, sometimes accompanied by their mothers or an older woman that very much resembled my grandmother but spoke in Nahuatl, my grandfather's language. I remember asking my grandmother why did the children have to work with their parents? Why did they have no shoes and their clothes were dirty or worn? Why did my grandma give them pesos on her way out of the mercado? My grandmother would reply with an "I don't know" or would just look at me and the sad gaze in her eyes and silence said everything. I did not understand a lot of things but I knew that money was essential for my family to have food on the table, and to share with those who were not as lucky as us when we had extra pesos. Little Maria knew that she had to do chores and homework to earn her pesos on Sunday. One day she would have enough pesos so that all the children and the grandmothers would not have to sell anything on the streets. They could be in their homes, enjoying a sopa de fideo, or a caldito de pollo, the way I always did with my grandmother.

I began to work at the age of sixteen. Being a young woman in a new country, not understanding credit and budgeting, I made some not-so-good decisions and developed some not so good money habits. I knew for sure that I had to work and work and work, just like mom and grandpa. There were seasons when I spent too much, and other seasons I saved as much as I could. When it was time to go to college, I did everything I could to find ways to pay for it, including getting into debt with student loans. Education was highly valued in my home because my grandparents were not able to go to school. My grandparents inspired me to love and care for school, to learn all that I could and read as many books as possible. I wish I could show you my collection of books. Back to my college story: during the first three years I got hit with the glorified access to a variety of credit cards. I remember banks having tables at the main student center and talking about how great credit cards were because you had access to an instant large amount of money. Credit was something you did not learn in the classroom. I did not know how to access and manage credit in a responsible way so I took out credit cards with high interest and fees. As a student with limited income, I had to pay the minimum payment every month and at the end I paid more money than what I had initially borrowed. After graduating with my bachelor of arts degree, I realized there was a lack of access to education on financial literacy. I leaned that the hard way. My debt grew with a few more student loans to help pay for my master's degree. But let me tell you, your personal and professional development is the one investment you will never regret. It will never lose its value.

After completing my master's degree, it was time to buy my first home. This time I had more information and I went to a housing counseling organization for pre-purchase counseling. I was able to understand what I needed to attain my home and to sustain my home. I did learn that my credit and savings were not where they needed to be, and I needed to do some serious budgeting and pay off some debt. Talking to other people in my community, I realized that many did not know where to access the resources I had, and that there were not only racial systemic barriers, but also cultural barriers. A few months of hard work paid off when I got the keys to my new home. I knew I had made my grandparents proud, and my kids would have a place to call their home.

We all have different values that come from our parents, our culture, and our unique societal experiences. Although many of us will have similar stories, each one of us is unique, and that is a very important key to remember when making your own budget and savings plan. Talking about finances is a very personal conversation, and I encourage you to never compare your story to anyone else's. As a financial coach, I serve as a guide for people to create their own financial goals and work on them at their own pace. I encourage my clients to build a new relationship with money, I help them develop an action plan that will lead them to attain their short and long-term goals, and to gain their confidence to take control of their own financial wellness. I also like to encourage people while setting their goals to come from a place of abundance, to picture as if they already have the house, the car, the vacation savings plan, the college savings plan or whatever their goal might be. I ask them to think of what financial wellness looks like for them. What does that feel like? Once they have that vision it is easier to set an action plan with attainable steps to achieve that vision. It really encourages people to create better financial habits, to feel empowered, to be self-aware and to adjust their plan as needed. I also make sure that they have access to good non-predatory financial services and home loans, so that they have choices and can make the right decisions for themselves.

Homeownership in this country is the vehicle to wealth, for people like me to be able to create generational wealth for our children. It is part of the physical legacy I want to leave my children with. Looking back at my financial journey, I think of the pesos my grandfather gave me was a little seed that was planted. Over the years I managed to water it, although sometimes forgetting and causing it to struggle. The little plant grew and started to set roots. Attaining homeownership meant those roots were now strong and deep, and the little plant had become a beautiful tall tree. Although there were times when hardships took a toll on the health of my tree, it managed to bounce back, time and time again. I got better at nurturing it, adding the right amount of water, and giving it the love it needed and deserved. I realize now that my life was always abundant. I had all that I needed to go through all the seasons in my life, all the fun and the not-so-great chapters in my story.

Use all of your experiences to make better road maps. You are the one in charge, and the only one who knows what is best for you. One thing that I want anyone who is reading this short story to know is that you, too, are abundant and you are the creator of your story. Invest in yourself, look for the resources you need to get through the rough times and to set yourself for success. I, too, am a resource for you, because I believe we all should have the opportunity to live an amazing life.

The fight for racial equity in all sectors will continue. My commitment is to continue to work towards closing the racial wealth gap one family at a time, one day at a time, making my contribution to creating healthy communities along with all the amazing people I have met during this journey across cities and states.

MY FINANCE INSPIRATION

Financial literacy is the knowledge needed to help you achieve financial wellness at different stages in your life. It does not have to start in a classroom, it can start at home, talking to your children, or parents, or partner about the values that influence your spending and savings habits. Learning to create healthy habits around money and credit can prepare you for bigger financial decisions that you will have to make in the future like buying a home, starting a business, and buying a commercial property or investing in real estate. Homeownership is the wealth-building vehicle in this country and serves as a path to creating generational wealth.

I encourage you to spend some time journaling on the questions below:

1. What is your first memory of money?
2. How has that shaped your relationship with money and finances?
3. How can you begin healing that relationship and disrupt the current system?

4. How can your healing contribute to create racial equity
    and generational wealth?

"The way to right wrongs is to turn the light of truth upon them."
— Ida B. Wells

BIOGRAPHY

Maria Ramos-Cuaya is a passionate and fierce non-profit leader, community organizer, and activist in the Chicagoland community. With the deep-held belief that every person matters, Maria is committed to helping individuals achieve success and reach their goals as they define them.

Maria is committed to leaving a legacy behind for her children and others. Maria's inspiration comes from her late indigenous grandfather, who told her: "One day when you feel you are successful enough to stand strong and continue to grow, turn around and get the next person to where you are, that is the only way you will contribute to making strong communities and changing the world."

Maria's passion for accessible education, family, community and culture has been shaped by her family's story and her own immigrant story as an undocumented child. This experience has birthed a heart for social justice, a desire to support others in their journey and informs much of the work that she does. Maria also can be found volunteering for The Young Center for Immigrant Children's Rights, where she acts as a child advocate, speaking up on behalf of and for the best interests of unaccompanied youth during detention and post-release, as a member of the Make-A-Wish Chicago Neighborhood Council, and board member of El Circulo Resource Center.

Maria has a bachelor of arts in Latin American and Latino studies as well as math and computer science. She also has a master of science in urban planning and public policy from University of Illinois at Chicago. Maria is a graduate of the Mujeres de HACE leadership program, a national program for high achieving Latina professionals. Following graduation, Maria gave back by serving as an alumnae board member on the program and event planning committee, which focused on planning and executing Mujeres de HACE programs and events to engage alumnae via professional development and networking opportunities, and to raise funds for scholarships.

In Maria's spare time, she enjoys discovering new places and food through travel, hiking, camping and exercising. She loves spending time with family and friends, taking long motorcycle rides with her life partner, and time alone reading some of her favorite books.

Maria D. Ramos-Cuaya, MPP
Non-profit leader, community organizer and activist
mramoscuaya@gmail.com
LinkedIn: @mramoscuaya

IF YOU FALL, GET UP AND PURSUE YOUR DREAMS

ARACELY MARKOWSKI

"This experience in finance not only helped me learn about the different financial programs that existed for mortgage loans, but it also showed me how much I could help my community given that there were many Hispanics who needed assistance in their native language, and I was there to guide and offer them my service."

My story begins forty-five years ago in the city of Quito, Ecuador. I am the youngest daughter of Jorge and Piedad Castro, and the youngest sister of five siblings who gave me lots of love, affection, and attention. When I was little, numbers would stand out to me, and my favorite subject was always mathematics. My interest in learning the topic of accounting was born from the fact that my father was a public accountant. In the Ecuadorian educational system, for the last three years of high school one can learn and graduate with a specialization in a didactic subject of one's choosing. I chose the subject of accounting, which I enjoyed greatly. I learned the fundamentals of this subject and became prepared for college in terms of making the right decision for what academic path to take. In 1995, I graduated from high school with a title in accounting; bringing this wonderful stage of my life to a close.

My mother immigrated to the United States and was able to apply for my residence. After graduating from high school, I was able to move to the United States, where the city of Chicago opened the doors to new opportunities and a unique way of life. The age of eighteen marked the beginning of a life of struggle and perseverance alongside my dear mom.

Immigrating to the United States was a challenging transition in every sense. The toughest challenge was leaving the rest of my family behind, given that we were very bonded to each other, and as I mentioned before, I received lots of love and affection being the youngest sister. I was no longer going to have them so close. It also was challenging leaving behind all the friends that I enjoyed and had shared so many beautiful moments of my life. On top of this, starting a new life in Chicago with the drastic difference in climate and seasons was difficult. I had never experienced snow and freezing temperature in Quito. Another challenge that was undoubtedly difficult was not knowing how to speak English. Despite all these challenges, I never lost faith in God, and with the company of my mother, we were able to move forward.

These next goals were the most relevant that marked my financial career.

The first thing I had to do was learn English and find a job. I signed up for afternoon English classes. A cousin of mine helped me to get my first job at an auto insurance agency, where I started filing client files, as it was the only thing I could do since I could not communicate with anyone. I have always put in the effort to learn, and I remember asking my co-workers how to say things in English, and how to answer the phone even though I did not understand. I would listen for the name of one of the agents to transfer the call to them, and if I did not understand at all, I would transfer it to any available person and, thus, lose the fear of speaking. Little by little I would progress and learn more tasks. My bosses saw my potential, my performance, and my desire to learn, so they decided to offer me the accounts receivable position where I could utilize my accounting knowledge.

I would take public transportation to work and to my English classes, and it was there when I had time to organize the plans and goals that I wanted to achieve.

The next goal was to buy my first car. Even though I did not know how to drive, I got the opportunity to buy a car, which then motivated me to dedicate time to studying for my driver's license. I went to take the driving test in my own vehicle, which I think should have been the other way around, but such was my motivation to get my driver's license. Having a license, being able to drive, no longer having to wait for buses, and not depending on anyone to give me a ride made me feel independent and free.

Although this may be insignificant for many, it was my push to continue setting goals for myself.

My next goal was to get a degree in accounting in the United States. This goal was particularly challenging given that I needed to know English. My desire to learn led me to find a college that gave me the opportunity to take basic general education classes, some of them being taught in Spanish, while taking English classes and advancing my proficiency in the language.

It took me four years to get my associate degree, longer than it takes most. The obvious reason was the language barrier. It was exceedingly difficult to work and to go to school full time. I hardly had a social life. But my focus and dedication paid off in 2000 when I got my associate degree in accounting and graduated cum laude, thus achieving the most challenging goal of my life.

My next goal was to become a financial loan officer for real estate mortgages. I had worked for almost nine years in the auto insurance agency, where I started without knowing any English, and where I gained the trust of my bosses. They gave me the opportunity to work, show my potential by mastering the language, gain experience in customer service as well as accounts receivable, and be able to earn a college degree, all during those nine years. I did not know what the future would bring, but it was time for a change. I accepted a new opportunity in a financial company where I could help my clients obtain home loans. This new job brought me great satisfaction since I was applying my mathematical knowledge; and at the time, the calculations were done manually. This experience in finance helped me to learn about the different financial programs that existed for mortgage loans, and it showed me how much I could help my community since there were many Hispanics who needed assistance in their native language. I was there to guide and offer them my service. In this season, I was able to buy my first investment building, manage the finances myself, and experience what it was to be a landlord. Unfortunately, the recession of 2008 came, and I was forced to look for a more stable job.

The next goal was to look for a job where I could show my full potential. After several weeks of job searching, I found an opportunity at a financial company. This company offered money transfer services to various countries, especially to Latin America. And with that, I was collaborating with my Hispanic community once again. My role at this company was territory manager for financial services; I managed the entire Illinois area. In this job I learned to work in management, technical support, customer service, and advertising. I collaborated directly with Hispanic owners of small businesses to promote our money transfer service and was able to build good relationships with agents, further promoting our services in this way.

While working in this company, I started a family. In 2009, I married my beloved husband, Tomasz Markowski. In this season of my career, I also had my two beautiful children, who are our motivation to keep moving forward. I worked in this company for almost nine years. It was a nice season; I felt fulfilled professionally and personally, always motivated to give my best in all aspects.

The desire to return to real estate and learn more arose in me. Here the next goal of my professional career was born: to obtain my real estate license. Working full-time with two young children did not stop me from achieving this goal. It was not easy, as I had to find the time to study while having a full-time job, being there for my family, and doing housework. I had to find a suitable place to concentrate and study, the only place being the library. In this period of several months, I hardly spent time with my children. Thank God, I had the help of my husband and my parents. I was able to get my real estate agent license in April of 2016. I passionately believe that if there is a will, there is a way, and you should always look for options to achieve the goals that you set yourself. There were many sacrifices and decisions that I had to make to achieve each important goal that I share in my story, as well as trusting and having faith in God. But the most important thing is to start dreaming and to never stop working for those dreams to come true.

In October 2016, I left my previous job, and from the day I decided to work as a full-time realtor, my new career has brought me much gratitude and satisfaction. I am once again helping my Hispanic community realize their dream of being homeowners and having their own space. Owning a home is the biggest financial endeavor one can have. I take my job very seriously as it comes with great responsibility in having to pay attention to the needs of each client. With the support of my husband, Tomasz, who obtained his real estate license to help me, we work as a team to provide an even better service to my clients. I also have my work team made up of loan officers, attorneys, home inspectors, and insurance agents. I know the magnificent work they do, and who I can recommend to my clients depending on their needs. In this way, I can find a way to help *everyone*, from clients who only have Individual Taxpayer Identification Number (ITIN) to those who are in the Deferred Action for Childhood Arrivals (DACA) program, even refugees with permits. My motto is. "Everyone deserves to have their own house."

In this season of my career as a realtor, I have promoted workshops in Spanish for first-time buyers where I give a step-by-step explanation of the purchase process and, in this way, educate my Hispanic community to make better decisions when they have the opportunity to buy. I also am honored each year to be invited to participate in Cicero School District 99's parent forums, where I inform and advise about the process of first-time home buying.

I actively participate in radio shows, community events, and small business events by bringing information and sharing tips for people to prepare for and achieve their goal of home ownership. The biggest reason I participate in these workshops and events is so that individuals have a notion of what the process is, and know that the opportunity exists for those who take it seriously and prepare. I manage my own publicity as well, putting to use all the skills that I have learned throughout the years.

I believe that the work I have done has borne much fruit, and there have been many happy and satisfied families who constantly refer me to their own family and friends. I feel very honored, blessed, and humbled to have received several awards including Su Familia Real Estate Top Producer of 2019, 2020 and 2021; Chicago Association of Realtors Top Producer of 2021; Homes.com and Homesnap's Excellence in Client Service 2021; Top 250 Nationwide from The National Association of Hispanic Real Estate Professionals (NAHREP) 2022; and Top 100 Midwest from NAHREP 2022. I am also incredibly grateful to have this job as it allows me a flexible schedule where I can enjoy time with my family and vacation with them, always having proper work-life balance.

I do not work only for recognition, but also to help families and those who seek my service. I thank all my clients and all the people who trust me, giving me the opportunity to guide them with my real estate knowledge.

Things do not happen overnight, you must persevere, focus, desire, and trust that if you fall you can get back up and move forward. Do what you like to do, and make sure to always have a balance between family, work, personal, and spiritual life.

MY FINANCE INSPIRATION

To be part of the finance world has taught me the importance of capital and money management. It provides an entrance to a path of opportunities where the different economic entities can benefit from the characteristics that finance has. The main objective is to achieve a correct administration of the money and capital to achieve good resources and achieve the proposed goals at the individual, family or corporate level.

Women need to feel fulfilled in the workplace and have the courage to pursue our goals and dreams. I know women's lives are full of challenges and we have many personal, family, and professional responsibilities. But the most important thing is to make smart decisions and look for the resources or people that can guide you to achieve your objective.

Personally, the reason that I decided to be a real estate agent is so that I could help and guide my clients to make a good decision on the biggest investment of their life, which is to buy a property. But to get to that point we must prepare our finances with:

- A good score credit.
- Savings for the down payment and reserves.
- Have at least two years of income taxes filled out.

Each case is different and if you need to improve some of these points, I can gladly help, guide or refer you to professionals who can guide you, like my book sister, Imelda Rodriguez, who is a financial coach - coachingvida21@gmail.com

BIOGRAPHY

Aracely Markowski was born in Quito, Ecuador, and she is the youngest daughter of five siblings. She has two sons and is married to Tomasz Markowski, who got his Realtor® license to help his lovely wife as a part time job. Aracely is a determined, dedicated, and motivated bilingual real estate broker who has seasoned sales and customer service experience for more than seventeen years. In 1995, she came to the United States after graduating from high school at the age of eighteen. Her first job was at Clover Insurance in Chicago, where she started filing the client files without speaking a word of English. With her determination and desire to learn, she gained the trust and admiration of her bosses, and after a few years was promoted to an accounts receivable position. In 2000, Aracely was able to achieve an associate degree in accounting, graduating with honors cum laude from St. Augustine College. She was also an active member of a youth group in Our Lady of Mercy Church, where her beliefs and faith in God got stronger.

Before becoming a Realtor®, Aracely worked in Unidos Financial Services as a territory manager in Illinois, where she earned a lot of experience in sales, customer service, tech support, management, and advertisement. She joined the real estate market in 2016 with many happy clients! Her desire is to help families to buy the home that fits their desires and their budget, as well as those that are selling their home to make the maximum profit possible. Aracely is an active promoter of first-time home buyer's seminars in the Hispanic community. She also participates in talk shows, giving advice and valuable information for future homeowners.

Aracely's hard work and persistence have awarded her multiple accolades including SuFamilia Real Estate Top Producer 2019, 2020 and 2021, Chicago Association of Realtors Top Producer 2021, and Homes.com and Homesnap Award for Excellence in Client Service 2021, Top 250 Nationwide from The National Association of Hispanic Real Estate Professionals (NAHREP) 2022, and Top 100 Midwest from NAHREP 2022. Aracely can balance between her professional and personal life, and enjoys worship, traveling, dancing, exercise, and family time more than anything else.

Aracely Markowski
www.aracelyhouse.com
aracely.sfr@gmail.com
Facebook and Instagram: @aracelyhouses

DIAMOND IN THE ROUGH

TIFFANY JIMENEZ

"I'll never forget the feeling, and the look on my children's faces as I opened the door to our first house. This was when I fell in love with the real estate industry, and what fuels my passion to want everyone to achieve the gift of homeownership."

O n March 30, 1983, a relentless warrior was born into a broken home. From the moment I took my first breath, I faced adversity. My parents had a toxic marriage and divorced when I was just a baby. When I was three years old, my mom married the best bonus dad a girl could ask for. The wedding was beautiful. I remember standing in my abuelas backyard in Juncos, Puerto Rico, in my white lace trimmed flower girl dress and admiring all the beautiful bright colored flowers and wedding decor. As the tropical sun shined on my face, I can recall the feeling of happiness I felt knowing now I had a family. Unfortunately, two years later my reality became a sad one when my mom and Sergio divorced. One of the things I'm most thankful for in life is the love God placed in Sergio's heart for me. It never wavered, still to this day he is a major part of my life, and I'll always be grateful, and Juncos, Puerto Rico, will always be my second home.

Choosing a career path in finance did not come as a surprise to my family. I am often reminded of a story of when I was six years old. My mom and I were driving past the car dealership in our older car and I said to her: "Why don't you buy us that nice new car? It's only $4.99." It was actually $4,999. That was my first lesson in numbers. I remember times when I wanted a new doll, Sergio would take me to the store to see the price. Then we would count how much I had saved, and he would help me figure out how much I needed to EARN doing small chores to buy it myself. Those experiences introduced me to budgeting skills. I still implement some of those same key skills in my business and with my own children.

School was where I excelled as a straight-A student, member of many clubs, and always ran for office. But when I became a cheerleader, I was given the opportunity to escape the reality of my broken home life, where I suffered abuse and lack of acknowledgement. I longed for my parents to be PROUD of me. Today, I understand they were facing their own demons and traumas. I am no longer angry or resentful and I am thankful for repairing the relationship with my father and continuing to work towards repairing the relationship with my mother one day. Although I experienced a childhood of absent parents, I have a lot of great memories with my aunts, uncles, and cousins. I remember having biscuits and coffee at my grandmother's house on Saturday mornings, cheering for my cousin, Jovani, as he played football, watching my tia's in the kitchen making tacos while my grandmother made her famous chile, and best of all, my prima Nicole letting me wear her clothes and use her makeup during our slumber parties. They truly filled the void of being an only child most of my life. I was truly blessed with the most amazing family, especially my tia's who stepped in to be my moms, I am incredibly grateful for the individual bonds I formed with them. My family showed me the true meaning of the saying: "It takes a village to raise a child."

At the age of fifteen years old, I had endured enough physical and emotional abuse at home and decided to move in with my boyfriend, Joshua, and his family. His mother, Diane, showed me what the love of a mother felt like. I will always cherish the bond we had. In November 1999, at sixteen years old I became a teen mom and introduced my daughter, Isaly, to the world. Being exposed to an abusive upbringing encouraged me to make the sacrifices needed for my daughter to have a two-parent home. When our daughter was seventeen months old, Joshua was murdered a block away from home. As he took his last breaths in my arms, I cried and I promised him that I'd give our daughter the life she deserved, a life filled with opportunities and love. After he passed away, I knew I needed to pursue a career that supported my vision and promise.

My first job was as a mailroom clerk at Illinois Vehicle Insurance. As a bilingual employee, I was able to work my way up to being a receptionist within months. Where I was able to learn the ins and outs of accounting. Soon after, a job opportunity as a bilingual accounts payable representative that offered better pay and benefits presented itself. I took a leap of faith and took the job. Although my life was filled with turmoil up until this point, I envisioned this job as a light at the end of the tunnel. But being subsequently terminated from a job I thought was secure gave me a new perspective of the definition of hopelessness. Now what was I going to do? I had no income, a daughter who depended on me, no rent money, and worst of all, my car was repossessed shortly after. To find employment, there were times I walked four miles with my daughter to her state-funded daycare where she was guaranteed two meals per day. Throughout this time, I remained focused on my vision and my promise and relied heavily on my village. I am thankful to have been blessed with my very own Golden Girls who played a major role in not only raising me but helping me raise my daughter into the strong woman she is today.

At nineteen years old, I met my son's father and I gave birth to my son, Nate, on July 3, 2003. Just after my twenty-first birthday, I became intrigued with the mortgage industry, with the idea of being my own boss and having a schedule tailored around my children. Being present in their lives was non-negotiable for me. One day I decided to call my best friend, Rosy Cordero, who was a loan officer, and asked her for guidance. After our call, I was ready to start my career in the mortgage finance industry. I spent some of the best years of my life at People's Choice Mortgage in Humboldt Park, a neighborhood in Chicago. The best thing about being chief executive officer (CEO) of your life is the power to control your time and it's something I am proud to have mastered. I was/am able to be present in my children's lives, never missing an assembly, field trip, or any of their extra-curricular activities while being a top producer. It truly was/is the best of both worlds. But, with two kids in private school, living expenses, and extracurricular activities, things were starting to take a toll on me financially. Having a "commission-only" career wasn't enough. I knew I needed a more secure income while I continued working on building my brand.

In 2005, I took my experience as a bilingual loan originator to a mortgage company in Roscoe Village, a neighborhood in Chicago. I didn't know it at the time, but the owner, Scott Tucker, would become a great mentor and advisor in the industry, and I can't thank him enough for all the knowledge he poured into me. I remember walking in for my interview and walking out with a salary job, a schedule that worked for my family, and the ability to originate mortgage loans. I knew I was on the path to building something amazing, a legacy I could leave to my children and that was my first step. Business was thriving and, at twenty-three years old, I purchased my first home in Portage Park, a neighborhood in Chicago. I'll never forget the feeling, and the look on my children's faces as I opened the door to our first house. This was when I fell in love with the real estate industry, and what fuels my passion to want everyone to achieve the gift of homeownership. The next couple of years were insane "in a good way." Business was thriving, I even ended up buying a processing company from a friend right before the 2008 real estate market crash. That's when it got real, guidelines started getting tighter and loans weren't funding. I found myself stressed out, in an abusive marriage, and struggling to keep up with daily life. From one night to the next, we closed our doors at the mortgage company in Roscoe Village, my home was in foreclosure, and I had filed for divorce. I felt as if the walls were closing in on me. I remember crying, wondering, where are we going to live, how was I going to pay for my children's school and extracurricular activities?' I was trying so hard to break the cycle and give them opportunities I never had, but that came with a heavy burden. Months after Scott closed his doors, he referred me to his friend, Perry Marshall, a Google Ads guru. In Scotts words, he said: "Perry needs Tiffany, a go-getter who brings solutions, not problems to the table." This is where I realized the value of hard work and business relationships. I was hired to work remotely for Perry's online company. Initially looking over failed payments, canceling memberships and collecting on past due monies. After two months, I moved into a full-time position, and just after one year I was given the opportunity to become a commissionable sales associate, where I've continued to earn a six-figure income working from home for the past fourteen years.

In March 2014, I gave birth to my third child, Victoria Grace. What should have been a happy time became a life of constant abuse. Here I was, a thirty-year-old mother of three, with a thriving career, suffering behind closed doors. I decided that I couldn't continue letting my children see their hardworking mother be abused. The day came where I had enough; I put a plan in place, dropped my children off at school, filed for an emergency order of protection, called the moving company, and never looked back. I would like to consider this the day I began to break the cycle I was born into, the day our lives would change forever.

For the first time, it was just me and my children. Isa was starting college; Nate was in high school while playing travel baseball; and Victoria was just starting preschool. That's when I decided to get my real estate license. Originally, I was worried about how time consuming it would be considering I had a full-time job, but also knowing I needed extra cash flow to offset college expenses. So, I took a leap of faith and a chance on myself. On January 15, 2019, after taking a two-week accelerated course, I became a licensed real estate broker. This was when I learned that betting on yourself is the best bet you can place. In all honesty, at my first showing I felt clueless. But, I was a quick learner with major confidence, a background in mortgage loan origination, and had navigated through one of the toughest markets in the history of mortgage finance. How hard could this new journey be? It's very hard work and takes a lot of dedication to be a top producing agent. Handing my clients the keys to their new home on closing day has been one of the most rewarding and lucrative experiences in my career.

One of the things I am most grateful for is the opportunity to break the cycle of abuse in my life. After finding true success in my careers, I finally also found success in my personal life. In 2019 surrounded by my village, I married Eddie Jimenez, the man of my dreams and my Number One fan. Not only has he taught me what unconditional love is, but he supports my ambitions and my dreams. He's shown me that I can have a successful career, AND a happy marriage, and that I don't have to sacrifice one for the other. I am incredibly thankful for the security that my marriage has brought to me and my family, and I look forward to continuing to pursue my dreams with their support.

Today, I am senior sales consultant and accountability coach with Perry Marshall Marketing, a top producing agent at Coldwell Banker Realty, an executive board member for the Chicago chapter of The National Association of Hispanic Real Estate Professionals, director for the Chicago chapter of The Women's Council of Realtors, a Chicago Association of Realtors D77 committee member, and a 2021 International Diamond Society Award winner. In my free time, I enjoy giving back to the community alongside my husband. We own and manage both a men's and women's softball teams and established a non-profit, R&M Athletic Association. We know all too well the benefits but also the extreme costs associated with organized sports, and the financial burden it places on families. Our goal is to bridge the gap and open the doors to organized sports to all, regardless of finances. My dreams have come full circle. I'm finally living the life I was destined to live. I wouldn't change any part of my experiences, especially all the challenges I faced. They have shaped me into the strong woman I am today, and I can't wait to see what the future holds.

MY FINANCE INSPIRATION

After becoming a single mother at seventeen years old. I knew I needed to take control of my

finances to provide for my daughter the life I had envisioned for her. As I became intrigued with finance, my goal was to be a top producer in the real estate industry. I was intentional

about surrounding myself with the right mentors and colleagues. I spent hours reading books and being coached. I wanted to learn everything I could from the best in the business. I was a quick learner and fast implementer, because I knew time was money.

If you are interested in becoming an entrepreneur and starting a career in finance or real

estate, I encourage you to make gratitude a part of your daily practice, find a great mentor, surround yourself with individuals who are positive, and those who have experience in the industry. I'd recommend joining the National Association of Hispanic Real Estate Professionals, and The Chicago Association of Realtors. Both associations provide valuable information to help you grow both personally and professionally.

Inspirational Reading:

- *Rich Dad Poor Dad* by Robert Kiyosaki
- *Think and Grow Rich for Women* by Sharon Lechter; authorized by the Napoleon Hill Foundation
- *The Confidence Code* by Katty Kay and Claire Shipman

BIOGRAPHY

Tiffany Jimenez is a bilingual top-producing real estate broker with Coldwell Banker Realty in Chicago's Gold Coast neighborhood. Tiffany is a serial entrepreneur with a strong background in mortgage lending and over twenty years of experience in the real estate industry. Tiffany understands navigating tough times and tough markets, which allows her to provide her clients with a comprehensive understanding of the entire real estate transaction.

Tiffany was most recently awarded the International Diamond Society Award at Coldwell Banker Realty, and serves as the executive secretary for the Chicago chapter of the National Association of Hispanic Real Estate Professionals. She is also a Chicago Association of Realtors D77 committee member, serving communities on Chicago's South Side. Tiffany is committed to educating future generations on managing finances and the different components of the real estate industry. When not assisting her clients, you may well find Tiffany fostering the spirit of philanthropy within her community, utilizing her not-for-profit to offer a safe environment for young men and women to build camaraderie, to spending time with her family and friends, sponsoring local food, coat drives, and educational seminars.

Tiffany Jimenez
www.tiffanyjimenezrealtygroup.com
tiffanyjimenezrealty@gmail.com
Facebook and Instagram: @tiffanyjimenezrealty

BE STRONG AND FIND A SOLUTION

MARY BUITRON

———

"If you don't like where you are, move. You are not a tree."

S ince I was a child, I remember my dad helping and caring for people; he was a doctor for the armed forces in Ecuador. I loved going to work with him at his office and pharmacy. His colleagues called him Doc, and I was Doctorcita (Little Doctor). Thanks to my father and mother, I had a life in our country full of love, affection, happiness, trips, walks, delicious meals, and lots of sports.

When I was fifteen, we decided to emigrate to Chicago, where my dad had some relatives. Although none of us knew English, everyone told my sisters and me that we would learn fast because we were young. Attending high school was the first step towards that.

I felt right at home at school as many classmates spoke

Spanish. Ever since I was a child, I have also liked geography, so I was happy to meet new friends from different parts of the world and realize that there were many people from Poland. I knew that Chicago had a vast Polish community, and although I hadn't learned English yet, I challenged myself to take Polish classes. A teacher told me I would not be able to understand it because I didn't even know English yet. Still, Ms. Urbanski, the Polish teacher, received me with open arms, without a care that I didn't speak English. I studied it for two years; I loved attending that class! I acquired a lot of the language, and every time I had the opportunity, I practiced it. I'm still learning that language that I love so much.

I had one disappointment among all the excitement of my new school and classmates. In Ecuador, I played basketball for seven years. I wanted to continue playing it. So I asked the school team if I could join, and that's when I heard my first "No" due to being short, thin, and not fluent in English. I decided to quit basketball and started playing soccer and chess.

When I finished high school, I wanted to go to university and study medicine to be a doctor. There I received another "No," because of my immigration status. I told myself, oh well, I'll look for an alternative. I became a medical assistant. When I graduated, my dream was to work in the big hospitals in Chicago and, little by little, grow in the medical field. However, once again because of my immigration status, I couldn't. I was getting used to hearing "No."

Therefore, it was a surprise that a doctor from India, Dr.

Molly Jacob, interviewed me, and was the first one to say "Yes." She hired me as soon as the interview was over. We worked in the pediatric area, where I learned much about the medical field. She also had a wellness, health, and fitness center. I have been passionate about sports since I was a child, so being there was wonderful. I will always be grateful to her for giving me that opportunity.

Working with children is fun; you realize that they enjoy everything and appreciate even the smallest of things. A little girl once asked me: "Why does that doll have hair and I don't?" I got a knot in my throat. From then on, I decided to donate my hair. Every two years, I cut fifteen inches and donate to children with cancer and leukemia.

I knew that I would move to Miami. Besides working with Dr. Jacob, I found a job in a nutrition and holistic products store. My friend, and store owner, John, has always been a blessing. Every time I have asked to work there, he has said "Yes." I worked both jobs for three months, seven days a week, as I wanted to save as much as possible before moving.

I lived in South Beach for about five years. Initially, it was hard as I didn't have my family or friends. I also didn't know the city. I bought a bicycle began to meet people and explore places. Sometimes I rode at 6 a.m., other times at 11 p.m. The bike was and is, until this day, my faithful companion. While living there, the Deferred Action for Childhood Arrivals (DACA) program started. A lawyer friend offered his services to help me fill out the documents that would grant me a Social Security card and a work authorization permit. I took a flight, arrived in Chicago, and we filled out the forms. I returned to Miami, and I received the documents that everything was approved in a couple of weeks. I still remember going on my bike to where they had to take my fingerprints and had a smile from ear to ear. Anyone would have thought I had won the lottery. For me, a girl with so many dreams but without papers, it was like winning the lottery.

After that, I applied for jobs without fear or shyness, knowing I had my documents in order. In my opinion, I was too old to study medicine. What a big mistake. Some people go to school when they are fifty, sixty or older.

There is a phrase that says: "If you don't like where you are, move. You are not a tree." It applies to relationships, friendships, jobs, etc. I identified with this phrase in a job I had, where I started loving it, but after almost two years, I said, I'm not happy anymore. I have to do something about it, and I have to do it now.

Many of my friends told me, "Mary, with your personality, your charisma, all the places you go, all the people you meet, you should get your real estate agent license. You will do very well." In one job, I saw how realtors helped many families achieve the dream of buying a house and how they helped their relatives financially. I said, "That's what I want to do. I want to help people who, like me, arrive in this country with many dreams, goals, and ideals, but for X or Y reason, we think we can't achieve them because of the obstacles that come our way."

For two months, I stopped working and focused on studying for the exam. Many people had told me that it was tough, so I dedicated myself to learning from the time I woke up until I went to sleep with the book on top of me. My dad has many certifications and diplomas, and he reads and studies every day; he is my greatest source of motivation. Also my mom, who, with her usual sweetness, supports my ideas that can be a bit nonsensical. Everyone in my family helped and encouraged me. Sometimes my little nephews made noise, and I couldn't concentrate. When they realized that I was studying, they became quiet. My dad offered to help me with math exercises; my mom told me I would pass because there was nothing that I couldn't shine in. My sister Lis said: "You can do it; you're smart." My boyfriend declared, "You're the person with the best memory. I know you'll do great." Everyone believed in me; I was the only one who doubted myself. I was also scared when thinking: "What If I pass and I don't get any clients?"

When I went to take the exam, they told me "No," because of my identification. The ID was valid, but the man in that office told me "No." I called my dad, crying, and told him I couldn't take the test. I felt so disappointed, sad, and bad; but as my dad taught me, you must be strong and find a solution. I called another location and scheduled my exam three days from then.

Two African-American women were there, and I asked them, please let me take the test. All I wanted to do was help families reach their homeownership goals and also help my dad financially so he could stop working. They became angels at that moment. They saw my ID and said to me: "Everything is fine; you can take the test." Hallelujah. One said: "I don't know what it means to be an immigrant, but my ancestors themselves were. Good luck with the exam." I sat in front of the computer, took three deep breaths, and prayed: "God help me; you know that I want this to help my family." Three hours later, I saw on the screen: Passed. If you ever took that test, you know what that means.

I cried, looked up, and said: "Thank you, God, I owe you one." I hugged the ladies there; I was shaking. I remember leaving the building on Michigan Avenue in Chicago and walking for about a mile. The whole way I was happily saying hello to everyone; maybe some people thought I was crazy. It was a mix of so many emotions. I was shaking, and I even thought I was going to have a heart attack as my heart was beating so fast. I told myself: "No, Mary, not right here in front of Millennium Park. You'll be on the news as "the girl who just passed her real estate exam and had a heart attack."

I love to eat with my loved ones, but I enjoy it when I eat alone. I sat in a lovely restaurant to celebrate with myself, and then I went to one of the free classical music concerts they do in the Pritzker Pavilion. The entire time I was smiling, being so thankful, and already planning how my life would change now.

As soon as I passed the exam, I texted my mom, dad, sister, boyfriend, and best friend. I then texted the managing broker, asking her when I could come into the office. I wanted to sign up right away and start working. When I received my license number and access to the system real estate agents use, I started learning, signing up for trainings every day, doing marketing, calling, and writing to everyone I knew with: "How can I help you?"

Once I heard one of the ugliest things. "People with an Individual Taxpayer Identification Number (ITIN) do not deserve to be given a loan in this country." In that moment, I wanted to cry and scream with fury and anger. I came to this country with an ITIN and got my documents thanks to DACA, but I will never forget how I started. I have had the pleasure of meeting several people with ITIN. They are very hard-working people; some even have up to three jobs. Many already have houses, investment buildings, businesses, and properties in their countries. They have their savings, comply with their taxes, and try to have everything in order.

I thought they deserved to have their home; for many, it is part of the American dream with which all immigrants arrived here. I dedicated myself to learning more about the subject until another angel crossed my path, my lender, Glenda. We started with a message from me on Facebook asking her: "Are you Ecuadorian?" From there, the rest is another story to be told.

I couldn't believe it when they invited me to be part of this book. I thought they had made a mistake about Mary. I asked myself what I would talk about if I didn't have much experience. I'm not a business owner. On the contrary, I also took it as a blessing, a drive, a challenge, and a learning journey. I chose to value and to appreciate this incredible experience that was presented to me.

I hope that those people who have been told "No" on several occasions can identify with my story. I hope that they do not give up, that they knock on other doors, and that they do not accept no for an answer. I hope that they know how to value themselves and, above all, value the people around them. Many of my compatriots have supported me and given me their trust, so I hope to offer my help and unconditional support back.

Since I was little, I have known that something I like is helping people. I've had the honor of being a volunteer at different organizations. From now on, my goal is to support and to educate everyone when I have the privilege to do so, especially immigrants like me, people who don't speak much English, have ITINs, and have been told "No." Proudly, I will always be a dreamer, as they call us DACA recipients. There are dreams that I hope to help my community achieve and, of course, fulfill some of my own, including working hard so one day I can tell my dad: "I did all of this because of you and for you."

MY FINANCE INSPIRATION

One of the two most significant motivations for entering the field of finance and specializing in real estate is my dad, whom I would like to provide with everything he has given my mom, sisters, and me all these years. I hope to tell him: "Dad, you don't have to work anymore. Rest and relax; I'll take care of everything."

My second reason is that I aspire to help those immigrants who, like myself, arrived in this country without speaking the language, without documents, without contacts, without knowledge, but who still desire to succeed and to create their American dream, their unique legacy.

I wish to educate families so that they can share the

knowledge with their children, and vice versa. I want younger generations to learn and to teach their parents, so that together we fully understand that we live in a country of opportunities. I want them to know that they can own houses, businesses, and investments. As long as they never lose the eagerness to learn, fight, work arduously, and strive for their dreams, the sky is the limit.

To the Latina women who want to enter the world of finance and real estate, we must not be intimidated. On the contrary, we should hold our heads high, carry our roots with pride, and above all, continue to prepare ourselves day by day.

BIOGRAPHY

Mary Buitron was born and raised in Ecuador. She moved with her family to the United States when she was fifteen years old. She was instantly fascinated with how cosmopolitan Chicago was, and the diversity of its people. Besides learning English, she studied a bit of French, Italian, Portuguese, and Serbian. Without a doubt, though, her favorite language is Polish. One day she hopes to master ten languages, so she can help more individuals in their native tongues.

She graduated from Wright College with an associate of science and obtained her medical assistant license from the Illinois School of Health Careers. She has always been dedicated to helping people, be it in her volunteer programs in nursing homes, children's hospitals, or citizenship classes for seniors. Now, she hopes to help her Latino community more.

Her goal is to tell people, "Yes, you can!" She hopes to hold their hand and guide them throughout the home-buying process, specializing in first time homebuyers and people with ITIN and DACA. Her focus is to provide the best service to those who want to sell their properties and teach people how to invest and generate income, all with compassion, honesty, and integrity.

Mary is a bilingual real estate agent, and a proud member of The National Association of Hispanics Real Estate Professionals. She is an avid reader, nature lover, traveler, and athlete who participates in triathlons and enjoys adrenaline-pumping activities, like skydiving.

Mary Buitron

(786) 474-0477

Marybuitronrealtor@gmail.com

Facebook: @MaryBuitron

Instagram: @marybuitron3

A BOLD DREAM

DENISE KROHN

"As a young woman in a culture that is predominantly male-dominated, I had to prove myself to my Latino counterparts and show them that I was capable of filling my father's shoes."

I was born into a loving family in the city of Chicago. The middle child, I was always the one that was caught between my brother and sister. Our parents were loving yet strict. We always knew that while home was a place that was safe and that you could run to, no matter the mistakes you made, you also knew that there would be consequences for your actions should you decide to take a less desirable route of action. We were brought up with strong Christian values, something that I am incredibly thankful for. My grandfather was a pastor, and so these values were instilled in us from a very young age, and they would eventually shape me into the person I am today. This combination of a faith-centered, loving, affectionate, compassionate, and strict-yet-fair upbringing created a foundation for an extremely happy childhood for me.

My dad immigrated from Cuernavaca, Morelos, Mexico at the age of fifteen. His father, who had come ahead, helped him and his two brothers to get their visas and get settled in the United States. He was a hardworking man, often working up to sixty hours a week with overtime to give us creature comforts that he did not have growing up. He met my mom, who had relocated from a small town called Guayama in Puerto Rico, when he was twenty years old. My dad joked that it was love at first sight, but my mom made him work for that first date! She began her journey in America at the age of eighteen, after tearfully leaving her mother to live with her brother in Chicago to send money home. As the baby in a family of seven, my mom felt it was her duty to take care of her mom after her father died at a very young age. The decision to leave her mom was one that broke her heart, but she faithfully sent money home for many years, allowing her mother to grow old comfortably in the childhood home she grew up in.

My mom was, and continues to be, a very devoted mother; always putting her children's, and now grandchildren's needs before her own. Even though we know she now struggles with health issues, she rarely complains, and instead will say: "I'm doing pretty good for an old lady." I've always loved her optimistic spirit, and I'm sure that I inherited mine from her.

My mother worked a morning shift, while my dad worked the night shift, alternating so that they could take care of us and not require outside childcare. Weekends were something that we treasured because it meant we could be together as a family. Saturdays meant sleeping in, cartoons, and my dad's famous pancakes. It's funny how I can still remember sitting in my onesie pajamas, sprawled out on the floor, watching cartoons on a remote-less television. I can still smell the sweet smell of maple-glazed bacon, while my dad cooked the most delicious pancakes. Sundays meant church, egg sandwiches for lunch, and usually the best steak tacos around (my dad's tacos were LEGENDARY!). I absolutely lived for all of this! I look back, and I am so grateful that my childhood was free of worries and free of any financial concerns—my parents had plenty. But they did a wonderful job of keeping us sheltered from them and free of any emotional concerns. I was so loved in my home and I was blessed with true friendships, many of which I still have to this day. We were free of any insecurities or anything that would bring a cloud to my sunshine. I now realize that this sense of security would lay the very foundation that would allow me to move on, to have the most ambitious of dreams.

Up until this point, my childhood and eventual teenage years were an incredibly happy time in my life. High school was a great time for me. I excelled academically and socially. Having joined softball my freshman year, and playing all four years, I made lifelong friends, many of whom continue to be some of my best friends today. As I neared graduation, I thought I had a clear-cut path for myself. I had always known that I would go to college, even though, at that point, not many people in my family had. I always knew that I was called to do greater things, though I did not yet know what they would be.

On September 3, 1998, my world came crashing down. My dad tragically died of a massive heart attack, without a moment's notice. He had complained a few days prior of a cold and said he'd had a slight pain in his chest due to coughing, nothing really out of the ordinary that would warrant a doctor's visit. It turned out that all along, he had been having mini heart attacks. Even though my mom had asked him to go to the doctor, my dad was never one to want to be a bother to anyone. So, he suffered silently.

I remember getting the call from my sister. It felt surreal, like someone had sucked the air right out of my lungs and I remember feeling lost about what the future would hold. The days after were a bittersweet combination of extreme sadness over my first real loss in life, but also a deep sense of gratitude over all the family and friends that rallied around us in support. This was also a time when my faith would become even further solidified, as I now felt I only had one Father I could cling to. I'll never forget the sense of peace that God gave me as a gift, as He assured me in my heart that everything would be okay.

My dad's passing was difficult for many reasons, but one of the most immediate issues that had to be addressed was the decision of whether we should keep or sell the family business. My father had been a businessman his whole life, self-taught but as hard-working as they come. He had worked a factory job with endless hours of overtime. Somehow, he always found time to dabble in different business ventures. He had a true entrepreneurial spirit, one that he passed on to me, and there were always new ideas that he wanted to follow. My poor mom had to constantly ground him and keep him from getting too carried away! She was always the more conservative one, concerned about maintaining a certain livelihood that would ensure a safe and modest lifestyle for our family.

At the time of his passing, we had a small grocery store, Los Portillo's, a fruteria y carniceria, in a predominantly Hispanic neighborhood. It was about two years old when he passed, and my mother immediately wanted to sell it. My twenty-year-old entrepreneurial self, however, would have no part in that! I would continue to run papi's grocery store and manage the employees. I would learn the inventory and payroll and all the ins and outs of running a small business. And I would fulfill my dad's dream and live out his legacy by building out this business into one of the largest *fruterias y carnicerias* in Chicagoland! At least this is what my twenty-year-old self truly believed, and I managed to convince my mom to give me a chance to run it.

At the time, I was a sophomore at DePaul University, and I worked part time at a bank. I adjusted my schedule so that I could get to a fruit market on the South Side of Chicago in my dad's old beat-up pickup truck at 6 a.m. I dropped off the produce and fruit, and opened the store by 8 a.m., letting in our employees who were there to help me with the day-to-day responsibilities and tasks. I would swing back around 2 p.m. and stay until we closed, helping with inventory, talking to vendors, manning the cash register, and eventually cleaning up. I'd go home around 10 p.m. and work on my homework until midnight or 1 a.m., only to wake up at 5 a.m. and do it all over again. It was exhausting, but equally invigorating, because I had a passion and felt I was living out this incredible dream for my dad!

Even though I had the best of intentions, the business was not doing well. We had extreme competition in the neighborhood, and I quickly found that while everyone was very nice to me as the owner's daughter, they somewhat resented me now that I was their boss. As a young woman in a culture that is predominantly male-dominated, I had to prove myself to my Latino counterparts and show them that I was capable of filling my father's shoes.

The one defining moment that I will always recall is my interaction, and eventual dissolution, with my butcher. The butcher was an older man, a machista as machista as they come. He was respectful to me at first, but eventually he treated me as if I were his inferior. He would not look at me when I talked to him, and many times would dismiss my suggestions and requests. One day, on a day that the cashier had called in and I had to skip school to open the store, we worked silently together, him preparing the meat for the day, me carrying in boxes from a delivery. He had no intention of helping me, and I had no intention of asking for help, even though the boxes were very heavy. The breaking moment came when I finally asked him to help me carry something, and he simply walked away and turned on the meat grinder to drown out my voice. Well, I'd had it! All that frustration came out in that moment, and I told him that he was a *"machista"* that didn't like to take orders from a woman, and *"Lárgese de mi tienda"* or "Get out of my store!" I stood there clenching my fists with my chin held high, knowing that I would always tap into this energy, any time I felt that someone in my life was abusing my kindness.

I wish I could say that this defining moment helped me to overcome all the challenges, that it would allow me to fulfill the outcome that I'd dreamt the store would have. It continued to lose money daily, money we could not afford to lose, and one day we made the very hard decision to close the doors. I will always remember this moment as the single biggest failure in my life! I had let my father down, and now would never fulfill this incredible legacy that I thought he left for me to fill.

That failure, however, would drive me to push myself to the highest limits. After graduation, I decided that I wanted to pursue business, but also wanted to make a deeper impact in people's lives. My father had let go of his insurance policy during the struggle with the grocery store, so there was no insurance money when he passed that would take care of our family. I decided to pursue Insurance, so I got my life and health insurance licenses, became an insurance agent, and adamantly tried to convince the world that every single person should have insurance. Yet again, the world was harsh and would not take this bright-eyed, inexperienced girl's opinion. So, I took my insurance licenses, jumped back into banking, and decided to dabble in investments. Here I got my Series 6 and Series 63 licenses, learning as much as I could about stocks and bonds. I genuinely believed Investing to be an incredibly important tool to create wealth, but again, the world did not want to take advice from this seemingly inexperienced young girl.

Eventually, I found my way into the world of mortgage lending, and I can honestly say it is my forte. I absolutely love helping my wide range of clients with their home lending needs. From the first-time homebuyer that is living paycheck to paycheck and wants to create wealth and opportunities for their families, to the investors that believe in creating homes in good communities for good families. Every single closing carries a very special place in my heart because I know that I have made a difference in someone's life.

I guess in a way, I am living out my dad's legacy after all. He wanted to make a difference in this world. He certainly made a big impact on mine. As a tribute to him, I have created The Alberto Portillo Hope Foundation. This foundation aims to help those that need a helping hand. From financial literacy workshops to food drives, the goal of this foundation is to help people that do not have the knowledge, education, or resources to create opportunities for themselves. My goal is to be a shining light of hope, and touch as many lives as I can.

MY FINANCE INSPIRATION

I was inspired to begin a career in finance after experiencing the financial turmoil that followed the death of my father. At the time, my father had chosen to forgo paying his life insurance policy because we had a struggling small business, and in his mind, the present was far more important than planning for the future. The aftermath of that decision was extremely difficult for my family, and it left us picking up the pieces for years.

Minority families are not often taught a basic foundation of how to manage their finances from prior generations. Considering that most minorities are first- or second-generation Americans, many are just starting off and are trying to find success in this country. Therefore, it is not paramount to plan for a rainy day or to invest for retirement, considering they are simply trying to get food on the table each day.

I decided that I wanted to go into finance to educate people with limited resources on how to manage their finances, for today AND for the future. I also wanted to inspire people to have a positive mindset and attitude that will help push them towards their financial and personal goals. Thankfully, through my work in various finance-related industries, I have had the privilege of helping many people; however, it is my wish to continue to focus on financial literacy through my foundation. My goal is to get in front of people earlier in the process (such as before buying a home, investing in stocks, etc.), with a deeper understanding of how to create a budget, save, and other fundamental financial concepts.

Books I recommend:
- *Think and Grow Rich* by Napoleon Hill
- *The 5 a.m. Club* by Robin Sharma
- *Psycho-Cybernetics: How to Tap into the Power of your Subconscious Mind* by Maxwell Maltz

BIOGRAPHY

Denise Krohn is a mortgage consultant that takes pride in helping her clients navigate through the challenging mortgage lending process. As vice president of mortgage lending at Guaranteed Rate, the third largest lender in the United States, Denise helps first time homebuyers and investors alike. As a top loan originator, performing in the top 15 percent of mortgage originators in the nation, she is committed to ensuring that her clients have a seamless lending experience. Furthermore, she is steadfast in educating and keeping her clients abreast of the constant changes in the mortgage industry.

Denise is not only passionate about real estate for her clients, but also about real estate investing for herself. She and her husband are unswerving in their devotion to create wealth for their children; thus, they are always looking for ways to grow their portfolio. As a mom of three young children, Denise understands the importance of investing now to set them up for success in the future. Denise is also a flipper, investing in urban and suburban markets, while also investing in short term rentals, like Airbnb.

Aside from real estate, Denise believes fervently in education and philanthropy. These are two key components of the mission of her foundation, The Alberto Portillo Hope Foundation. She is committed to unceasingly creating opportunities to educate people on financial literacy issues, while continuing to support underprivileged neighborhoods. Denise is hopeful that this book will continue to open doors that will allow her to encourage minorities, especially young women, to take bold steps that will create generational wealth.

Denise Krohn
denise.krohn@gmail.com
Facebook: @Denise.portillokrohn
Instagram: @Denise_Krohn

BEAUTIFUL LATINA MIND

MARTHA RAZO

"Mathematics is the language with which God has written the universe." —*Galileo Galilei*

A CLOSED DOOR LED TO MY GROWING LOVE FOR NUMBERS

My story starts with a closed door! I've always been optimistic and found my own doors. In high school, knowing that I was undocumented, I did not let that stop me. I was constantly told by peers and counselors to not work so hard, that I'll end up working in a grocery store or factory. However, I sought out answers. I was told because I was undocumented, I could not go to college. After talking to many community leaders and experts in immigration rights, I discovered that I was able to go to college.

I took a step further and partnered with Universidad Popular to raise funds for undocumented students. My team included other high school students from different schools. We started Students for Students, for which we were able to award a total of eight scholarships between $500 to $1,000 to undocumented students.

However, the steam to my train stopped when it was my turn to apply for college. I have wanted to be an actress since I was young. I loved being on stage. I was even the master of ceremonies at only ten years old when I was at Edwards Elementary School.

I was accepted to a top theater school in New York; only ten students that auditioned in Chicago were selected. I was one of them! But my dream was quickly shattered. I called to ask about funding to pay for tuition. When I called the financial aid office and told her I was undocumented and wanted to know if there were scholarships, I was interrupted and yelled at by the financial aid office. "What are you doing in our high schools? You should not be in our schools. Go back to your country."

I was devastated. I stopped. I completely stopped going to school. I stopped doing any assignments. I remember sitting across the table from my worried mom. I remember my mom asking: "When are you going to school?" I would respond, "Mom, I am safer here. I no longer find the reason to continue living." Yes, I thought of taking my life many times. For me at that moment, it was not worth living anymore. My dream was always to go to college. I dug myself into a deep hole for an entire school semester.

I finally got up from my dark depression when my counselor

warned me that I would not be graduating high school since I needed four years of English credit. Was I going to throw away three years of hard work? I had straight A's my first three years of high school, and now I was failing all my courses with lower than 40 percent. I decided that I had enough of pitying myself. I had to get out of the hole and finish high school, graduate, and accomplish my goals.

I am thankful for the support of two amazing women who guided me and led me to get into college.

First and foremost, Sofia Villafuerte, who was the college counselor at Marie Sklodowska Curie Metropolitan High School in Chicago. She helped to give me hope and to apply to college. I had put aside my acting career. I didn't know what else to do. I always enjoyed mathematics. So, I chose to major in applied mathematics.

Then there was Tanya Cabrera, the assistant vice provost for student inclusion at Illinois Institute of Technology (IIT). Tanya guided me from the scholarships to the different programs offered. I was admitted to twenty colleges. I began my bachelor degree in applied mathematics at IIT in the fall of 2012. This was the beginning of my pursuit for my passion in mathematics, and my growing love for numbers and data.

I had a new mission! I was now going to apply for my mathematics degree and learn all aspects of mathematics, education, corporation and research. And I did. I even made numbers for my own business. I will get to that story at the end.

MATHEMATICS IN EDUCATION

I minored in mathematics education at IIT. I wanted to be a teacher in mathematics in high school. I realized that many of my peers in college dropped out or switched majors because they struggled with calculus and other college math courses. It was heartbreaking for me to see that some of my Latino peers who dreamed of being engineers or doctors gave up on their dreams for calculus.

I wanted to change that. I had love for math and hoped that it would be contagious or would at least bring some light of understanding to students. Maybe I could be the changing factor for them to pursue their career goals.

I was a teacher for geometry and algebra at Back of the Yards College Preparatory High School for a semester. I quickly realized that teaching was just not for me. I loved the students and, of course, mathematics. However, the politics in the education system did not allow me to make an impact on students the way I wanted.

MATHEMATICS IN CORPORATE

I went to the next path in mathematics; I went into corporate. I was given the opportunity to intern at Barclays headquarters in New York in 2016. I was the only Mexican intern. I was a data analyst in the technology department of Barclays. I was able to use everything I learned in my applied mathematics studies at IIT. I built mathematical models to forecast the sales revenues of clients that used Barclays business tools. I analyzed relationships between client use of Barclays resources and revenue. I was even given the opportunity to teach my supervisors techniques for analyzing data and statistics tools I used for modeling. I developed a four-week curriculum for my supervisors and gladly shared my knowledge.

Besides developing models and analyzing data, I conducted assessments of various business intelligence tools and mobile solutions. I helped in the decision-making of which business intelligence tools were most appropriate to support Barclays' goals.

I learned about many BI tools, how to assess them. I was even given the opportunity to lead a demo session on new technologies Barclays adopted in their corporation. I was offered to stay full time for the fall of 2016. I was honored and delighted. I wanted to stay at Barclays. I had an amazing manager who I wanted to continue working with. However, back home in Chicago was my family. I left my home when I was only eighteen years old. I did not want to leave them again. I declined the offer and decided to come back home and focus on building and growing my parents' business, Guero's Pallets.

NUMBERS POWER TO GROW GUERO'S PALLETS

I came to the company my father started back in 2004 and incorporated in 2006. My father had started this company from humble beginnings, with a hammer in his hand and a desire to get us out of poverty. I started working in 2014, as I was obtaining my bachelor's degree. I would go to school, come to work, and then go to my evening's courses. It was not easy, but it was worth it. My efforts paid off. I graduated in 2017 with no school debt and with two degrees, a bachelor's and a master's in applied mathematics from IIT.

Using the power of numbers, my data analytics tools, I was able to prove to the bank that Guero's Pallets was able to pay off a loan for a property. In 2016, we were finally approved! We moved the entire company to our own warehouse in the heart of the Chicagoland area. Expansion was even more possible with our 2.75 acres of land. I brought all I learned from my father from business, from my mathematics degree, my experience teaching, and working in corporate, and started developing strategy and plans to build our family company.

My first plan was to better understand the market. I studied the market profoundly. I also started analyzing financial reports and started to understand where we were overspending and opportunities to grow our revenue. I was able to develop forecasting models that allowed us to not only project our sales and profits, but understand what variables influenced our growth the most. At the beginning of each year since 2017, I began creating yearly plans. I then had monthly financial, production, and inventory reports for each month. I used these reports to guide my strategy and action plans for every month. With time our business became more independent from brokers; our sales increased and with that our profit margins.

Even during the pandemic, we came strong, because any decision I had to make I went back to the data. Alongside is the leadership of my brother, Rafael Razo, who oversees all warehouse operations; the help of my brother, Juan Razo; my father, Agustin Razo, and my mom, Maria Razo, who are working day and night making sure that every detail in operation is attended to. My sister, Ruby Razo, helps manage our accounts receivable. It is really a team effort, guided by the power of numbers, that has led to our unimaginable growth. We will have over $14 million in sales in 2022, and we are blessed to continue growing and expanding.

THE BEGINNING OF INDUSTRIAL ENGINEERING

The survival of any business in the future will be dependent on how well they use their data to create business strategy! This is a serious phrase, and feel free to quote me in the future. I realized that the growth at Guero's Pallets was a combination of hard work and allocating resources strategically, using the answers behind the data and numbers. I decided to pursue my PhD in industrial engineering, with a focus on data and process mining.

I did not believe it; but I was admitted and am blessed to be funded as a researcher at University of Illinois Chicago (UIC). I have collaborated on several published papers in process mining in the medical field. My publications can be found in Google Scholar. My current work at UIC is a prediction algorithm called Adjacency Matrix Deep Learning Prediction Model (AXDP), which predicts the next event in a system, such as a business process.

I also was given the opportunity to develop a prediction model to help increase the number of cardiac arrest patients that survive. I am in the beginning phases of this research project, but I am optimistic that the findings will help save lives and help medical experts make optimal decisions for treatments for patients with cardiovascular disease.

I will be done with my coursework in May 2023, and will finish my thesis one year after that. Pursuing my PhD has not been easy; it is challenging every day. But as in anything I do, I never quit. I am focused, and I work hard. I know that all the techniques and tools I am learning in analyzing data, I will be able to bring back to Guero's Pallets and keep expanding our business.

My love for data and numbers led me to my new venture, and that was to start my own consulting firm to help business owners grow their business using their data.

THE POWER OF NUMBERS WITH SOLIX

Business is a numbers game. To be in business and to survive for many years, it is important for a business owner to know and UNDERSTAND the business numbers.

During the pandemic, more than ever, we saw how volatile business owners are to market shifts and external factors. According to the Journal of Economics & Management Strategy from January 2020 to June 2020, there were over 3 million businesses that closed their doors due to the pandemic. Watching the news and listening to stories of the families affected by the closures brought me to tears. While these businesses were closing, ours was growing. We were not lucky; we were doing something that worked. That is when I realized that there was power in the numbers.

I decided to open my consulting firm. I made it my new life's purpose to help small business owners to stay in business for the long run and to grow their companies using data-driven decisions. I started with my six-week course called The Power of Numbers. The first cohort of students graduated on November 19, 2022, and they presented to investors and bank lenders. I referred to them as the Cobras, a small twist to the Shark Tank show.

In The Power of Numbers six-week course, I teach business owners exactly what I did to build a multi-million-dollar company. I teach business owners the key numbers to create business strategy, the important financial reports, and how to read the financial reports. I also teach how to create a budget to lead a proactive business strategy and to use forecasting to plan for expansion.

My students get to use the calculators I developed for forecasting and calculating the break-even price. In changing markets, such as those resulting from a pandemic and a recession, prices change, and those businesses that do not change their pricing accordingly and on time can find themselves in financial hardships. The calculators address that issue, and the students learn how to use and to apply the calculators, and to create a strategy that builds their business foundation for even the strongest of storms.

In my consulting side of Solix, I emphasize three important metrics or pillars: financial, marketing, and operations numbers. I guide business owners in understanding and having these metrics align when creating their business strategies. I help business owners allocate their resources efficiently, develop budgets, create forecasts and apply those forecasts, and calculate break-even prices. For mid-size and large companies, I provide process optimization of their production and management.

In simple terms, I use business data and convert it to dollars in their pockets. So, what is next for business owners when they grow? The next is investing. Where do they put their money to grow it? This leads to another hat I wear in the finance-and-numbers world—helping families build generational wealth.

BUILDING GENERATIONAL WEALTH

In 2022, I joined World Financial Group to help families build wealth. My objective with World Financial Group is to educate the younger generation to start saving for the future.

Interestingly, it is through vehicles, such as life insurance, that one can also invest to grow their investment. Unfortunately, many people do not understand how these investments work.

I teach the power of seventy-two, compound interest, and saving in taxes and investments. Becoming a millionaire is not impossible. It takes using the power and rules of numbers.

My mind is not just numbers. I am a mother to an amazing son, Angelo Vazquez, who I know is watching me. I want him not to follow my footsteps. Instead, I want him to realize that everything and anything is possible. What really matters in this life is to live your purpose and do what makes you happy and fulfills you.

MY FINANCE INSPIRATION

The Federal Reserve reports that 36 percent of Americans don't have enough money on hand to cover a $400 emergency. That is over one-third of the population. Also 51 percent of Americans have $5,000 or less in savings. Now in the business world, a recent study by the U.S. Bank analyzed the reasons small businesses failed. In their study, they found that 82 percent of the time poor cash flow management or poor understanding of cash flow contributes to the failure of a small business. It is clear that as a nation, we have poor management of finances. There is a need for education across our nation. Families are being broken due to financial problems. Closing businesses are leading to employees being out of work. Financial problems lead to stress and can even lead to health problems in the long run.

I have made it my mission to help others build wealth, one number at a time. I will dedicate my life to impact the lives of others, to help them build wealth. The finance industry is growing. Finance professionals are in high demand. Furthermore, if you are a finance professional, you are able to impact generations of lives. You can liberate others from financial burdens, through education and information that can change their lives forever.

I am passionate about numbers, and every day I am happy and fulfilled to know that I am changing someone's life and impacting their family at the same time. If I can help a business grow, I have opened doors to others. If I help someone understand their finances, I have helped them open doors to their success!

There is no better gift than that of helping others find their success and realize they are limitless.

BIOGRAPHY

Martha Razo is a writer, mathematician, engineer, pallet expert, actress, philanthropist, entrepreneur, and co-CEO and co-founder of Solix Services. She believes that with data-driven solutions a company can achieve real growth. Martha experiences the power of data in her own work at Guero's Pallets, Inc., where she oversees daily operations as CEO. Martha has a bachelor's and a master's from the IIT, and she is currently pursuing her PhD in industrial engineering at the UIC with a focus on data mining and process mining.

Martha is the founder of the 2% Fund, a nonprofit whose mission is to increase undocumented students enrolled in higher education through financing and mentorship. In 2019, she co-authored My Dream Fund, a one-woman show about her story and how she overcame barriers as an immigrant to become the successful entrepreneur and educated, powerful woman she is today.

Martha has eight years of business experience and over six years of experience analyzing big data and artificial intelligence. She brings tools for interpreting and analyzing business data and a strong foundation of what it takes to run a business. Her publications can be found on Google Scholar.

Martha Razo
(312) 523-5561
www.martharazo.com
www.solixservices.com
solixbizservices@gmail.com

I AM THE ATTORNEY

NANCY PIÑA-CAMPOS

"It seemed unrealistic to me to start a new career at thirty. My brother responded, "That's true, but you will eventually be thirty anyway. So, you will either be thirty and still be the assistant to the attorney, or you will be thirty and you will be the attorney."

College. Beginning of senior year. What am I going to do with my only one and precious life? Am I too late? Shouldn't I know by now? The pressure was on. I hoped we were all in the same boat, so I decided to ask the guy next to me what his plans were. "Law school," he said. How amazing, I thought. I am sitting next to someone who will one day be an attorney! He must be so smart and his parents must be so proud. I remember wishing I could do that, but not for a second did I think I actually

143

could. Why? Why not me? I was in the same exact class in the same exact university as this person, and yet I didn't even think it was an option for me. I don't know where the doubt stemmed from, but it wasn't until many years after college that I realized that I was smart enough and powerful enough and capable enough to achieve my dreams. From that moment, I have never looked back.

The history of my family is no different than so many we know and those who came before us. My father came to the United States to look for an opportunity to provide a better life for his family. He left my mother and brother behind in Mexico for a year until he had at least found a job and a place to live, and then he brought them, too. My father grew up poor and only made it to fifth grade. My mother only finished the third grade, and then it was time to work and help raise her brothers and sisters. Despite the hardships, the sacrifices, and their limited education, my parents managed to achieve success beyond what was thought possible. My father started sweeping auto repair shop floors while also taking classes to be a mechanic. My mother worked in a factory during the evenings and took English classes during the day, while also caring for the home and raising my brothers and me. Eventually they opened their own auto repair shop, which has been in business for over forty years. Although my parents didn't have an academic education to lean on or to pass on to us, they had something much more valuable—grit. Grit is having courage and resolve. It is the sheer determination to succeed, to achieve your goal despite the setbacks, despite the fear, despite the unknown. Grit is something that cannot be taught in school. But it's something that comes deep from within your heart, and my parents passed this on to me by example.

Growing up I knew I was going to go to college. There was never any question about that. I knew what my parents had gone through, what they had sacrificed and how far they had come, and I knew they had done it all for my brothers and me. They had worked way too hard for me not to succeed. So, college was a no brainer, but then what? I used to think I was raised to believe I could do anything I set my mind to, but it wasn't until years after that moment in college when I realized that something had been holding me back. Deep in my subconscious I didn't really believe I could do anything. Perhaps it was because I had never seen a woman who looked like me have a certain position or career, and without knowing it, the glass ceiling was also holding me back.

I graduated with a degree in real estate investments and finance, and after college I took a job in a real estate investing company, analyzing commercial properties and figuring out the best rate of return. At first, the investors were only investing in real estate. After a while, the owner of the company opened a different department and started asking his clients to invest in stock for the company. People trusted this man, and it turned out to be a Ponzi scheme of unimaginable magnitude. His target clientele was Hispanic men and women business owners, including my own family. It was devastating beyond words to find out what he did to these people. I had never seen so many grown men cry. Whether they had invested $500,000 or $25,000, it was their entire life's savings, in many cases. It was the money they had worked so hard to save, the money they hoped to retire with, or the money they planned to pay for their children's college education. Just like that, it was lost. These investors were not all savvy, experienced, or wealthy investors. Many simply had worked hard their entire lives, sacrificed, and saved enough where they wanted to take the next step to make their money work for them. It didn't turn out that way, and that man ended up in prison, where he belonged.

It's still painful for me to relive those moments, and I always regret not knowing it was happening so I could try to prevent it. It was definitely a turning point in my life. It brought a realization to me that if these people had had adequate representation, such as an attorney who truly was looking out for them and who spoke their language, something like that may have been avoided. Up until that point I had never imagined that I could be an attorney. Attorneys were men. They were white. They were over fifty years old. At least that's what an attorney was in my mind.

I never thought I could not be an attorney. I never thought I could be an attorney either. This is because it was never a question that I asked myself. It was something I had never even dared to dream. That glass ceiling was still very much above me. The closest I thought I could get to this dream I didn't even know I had was to work for an attorney. So that's what I did. I worked for a law firm that specialized in foreclosures and repossessed residential property, also known as real estate owned (REO). All day long, I reviewed real estate files and prepared closing documents. It was then that I felt that maybe, just maybe, I could be an attorney.

By this point I had been out of college for about five years, and the thought of going back to school was daunting. So, I decided not to. I remember telling my brother, "I'm thinking of going to law school, but by the time I graduate I will be thirty years old!" It seemed unrealistic to me to start a new career at thirty. My brother responded, "That's true, but you will eventually be thirty anyway. So, you will either be thirty and still be the assistant to the attorney, or you will be thirty and you will be the attorney." That response made all the difference. How many times have we held ourselves back because a task will take too long? We avoid it altogether when, in reality, the time will pass anyway. Time is certain.

I went home that day and made my plan. I literally made a vision board. I did my research and I wrote down the law school I was going to attend, the score I was going to receive on the LSAT, the year I would graduate—everything was on that board. While other young adults were visiting law schools with their parents, I was visiting them with my husband. It was my first year of marriage and more than once we were told that the divorce rate among law students was very high. We were told it was going to be a high stress environment and so much work that we would rarely see each other. We didn't know it at the time, but it would end up being very true. During those years we were also dealing with the aftermath of the great recession so it was a very difficult time financially. It would have been helpful to have two incomes, but my husband never questioned my decision to go to law school. Instead, he encouraged me and supported me financially and emotionally every step of the way.

Law school was every bit as stressful as they said it would be, but we survived. It was so intense and there were many students who dropped out the first and second year. But I had not come this far to quit now. And yes, many of the students were white males, which matched my idea of what an attorney looks like, but I was pleasantly surprised to see more and more of every kind of person: African-American, Asian, a few Latino, and women! A lot of women, which was so amazing and wonderful to see.

During my last year of law school, I was pregnant with my first son. He was born on May 8. I was actually in the hospital the day after giving birth and finishing up one of my final papers. Ten days later was graduation and my newborn son was in the audience watching me receive my law school diploma (actually, he was sleeping, but the point is he was there). The next two months were beyond exhausting, but this precious baby was my motivation to get through the long days in the library studying for the bar exam, and the long nights with a newborn. The bar exam was in July and it was two full days of testing. We needed a new word for "stressful" to describe what it was like, because that doesn't even begin to cover it. Two very long months later, in October, the results arrived by email. My baby was on the couch peacefully asleep, and my husband was at work. I saw the email had arrived and so I said a prayer before I dared to open it. I took a deep breath…."Congratulations…" That's it. That's all I was able to read. I fell to my knees and cried. Oh, how I cried. I cried tears of joy, of relief. Tears of gratitude and even tears releasing frustration. All the feelings I had felt during the past ten years were released from my body in the form of tears. It had all been worth it.

I worked for a couple firms at first, because I wanted to get a feel for different areas of law to find what I really wanted to practice. I handled immigration law cases, family law, criminal law, and bankruptcy. Ultimately, I knew I wanted to return to my first passion—real estate. So I opened my own law firm. As an attorney, I represent buyers and sellers in commercial and residential real estate transactions. As a Latina attorney, I feel so honored to be able to represent hard-working Hispanic men and women in what often is one of the biggest purchases/investments of their life, and I am so proud to be able to do so in their language.

To the woman reading this... don't doubt yourself. Regardless of your background, your upbringing, the point in your life where you are today, and regardless of how long it will take to achieve your dreams, know that you are powerful and capable and deserving. We, as women and women of color, have a right and a responsibility to take our place in this world in whatever field we choose. We have a duty to pave the way for the next generation just as the women who came before us have done. It's okay if we don't see other people who look like us in our chosen field. It doesn't mean we can't, it just means we must be among the first. I have been an attorney now for almost nine years, and still today I may show up to represent my client in a closing and the receptionist will say: "Sit down and wait for your attorney." I don't get offended; they just don't often see attorneys who look like me, either. I simply have to say, "I AM the attorney."

MY FINANCE INSPIRATION

Money can't buy happiness. Yes, most of us know this to be true. But it can certainly buy financial freedom and that can lead us on the pathway to achieve the things that bring us true happiness.

The term "finance" can be very broad, but part of its meaning is the management, creation and study of money and investments. It's very important for all of us to not only have money for living day to day, but understanding how money works and how we can make it work for us so that we are not living day to day, paycheck to paycheck. To achieve financial freedom means that we are not worrying about where our next paycheck will come from, how we will pay the bills, or how to keep ourselves from the things we want to do that truly bring us happiness, such as traveling to see the world or having the luxury of spending more time with our children.

It is particularly important, more than ever, for women to grow and expand their financial knowledge to gain independence in every aspect of their lives. As the quote says, "Here's to strong women. May we know them, may we be them, may we raise them."

BIOGRAPHY

Nancy Piña-Campos is the founder and owner of Piña Law Firm, LLC. Her practice focuses on real estate transactions. Nancy graduated from DePaul University with a major in real estate investments and finance and she obtained her juris doctor from The John Marshall Law School. While at John Marshall Law School she was president of the Real Estate Law Student Group, member of the Latino Law Student Association, member of Lambda Alpha International (Honorary Society for the Advancement of Land Economics) and member of the Trial Advocacy Honors Council. During this time, she also held an externship with the Neighborhood Housing Services.

Nancy's other work experience includes work as a judicial extern for The Honorable Lisa Marino of the Circuit Court of Cook County, Chancery Division, as a legal intern for Clarion Associates conducting research for the Argentinian Conservation Easement Project, and volunteer at the Domestic Violence Legal Clinic. Nancy is licensed to practice law in the state of Illinois and is fluent in Spanish. She lives with her husband and three beautiful children.

Nancy Piña
attorneypina@gmail.com
(773) 314-7788
Facebook: @pinalawfirm

LIFE HAPPENS FOR ME, NOT TO ME

EVELIN F. FREYTAS

"But my family questioned, how could I go from a six-figure salary to 100 percent commission after so much sacrifice and hard work? My answer was easy, our communities deserve more. I was no longer choosing a career for the money but rather following my new personal mission."

B eing born and raised in Quito, Ecuador had its perks: great weather, delicious food, and most importantly, my loving family. My mom is the third youngest of twelve children. She was only seven years old when my *abuelo* died, and at that young age, she had to figure out ways to help contribute financially. She instilled a work ethic full of love. She worked multiple jobs to make sure that I had clothes on my back, but also the best experiences, and most importantly, the best education. She believed that education was the way out of poverty, so she enrolled me in a private school. To afford the tuition, my mom, Suzy, was living paycheck to paycheck, borrowing from one individual to pay another. In addition, as a single mother with no financial help, she had to move us into a one-bedroom apartment. By one-bedroom, I mean our entire home was an 8-by-10 bedroom. It only fit a full-size bed, which I shared with my mom, a small stove in the corner, and an outdoor communal bathroom. That was our life and the challenges that came with financial insecurities.

There was a reason it was just Suzy and Evelin; just the two of us. My father was absent. His absence was not ideal, but necessary. One of my most ingrained memories of my father is that he made it very clear that he preferred a boy instead of a girl. That made me feel like I was not good enough. He felt I was unworthy to carry on the family legacy. My earliest memories were of him hitting my mother with an ironing cord and me jumping in front of my mother to protect her. She tried to endure the domestic violence and work things out with him so I could have a "family," but it was not safe. One summer morning when I was four years old, I was taking too long to eat my oatmeal, according to my father. After asking me multiple times to hurry up and eat, to no avail, my father lost it and pushed my face into the oatmeal bowl. It was my mom's turn to step in to protect me, and she did. She begged him to stop and asked him why he was being so mean to me and my father yelled something that would forever shape my life. Without any hesitation, he screamed, "I didn't want a girl, I wanted a boy!" and walked away. That was the last time I saw my father.

After many years of financial insecurity, things started looking positive. When I was nine years old, we were able to move to the United States, although the journey was not easy. A year prior, my mother embarked on the trip before me, and unfortunately some complications arose. The one week apart that we had originally planned for turned into a year under my aunt's care. Although I was surrounded by my loving family, I felt like an orphan for that entire year without my mother. But I remained hopeful. My mom came back for me and we made the journey back together. While in the United States, my mom remarried. I finally had what I'd always wanted, a loving family and financial security. There was my loving stepfather, an amazing stepbrother, a dog, and a home in the suburbs. Due to my stepfather's job, we moved around a lot. I lived in Schaumburg, Illinois; Scottsdale, Arizona; Delaware, Ohio; and finally back to Schaumburg. To fund a Washington, D.C., class trip in junior high school, we were given order forms and gift supply kits to sell door-to-door. I became the top seller with an excess of $2,000 in profit to spend on my trip, and that is where I began to cultivate my business skills.

Unfortunately, during my senior year in high school, my stepfather sat me down and told me that my parents were getting divorced. It was so unexpected since I always believed they had a loving marriage. As he hugged me and said he loved me, one of the last impactful phrases he left me with was, "take care of your mom; she really needs you right now." I needed her too, we needed each other, and this shaped all my decisions since that moment.

My life changed, and the next day I applied for my first job to help support our family. I was sad to miss out on school events and spending time with friends, but I was grateful one of those jobs would be with the ALDO shoe store. ALDO was the job where I found my first success in sales. After a few months, I won the Club Elite award, which included an all-expense paid trip to Canada to meet the founder, Mr. Aldo Bensadoun. As a high school student, this experience was so impactful. I went on to win that award three more times and, as a result, I had an opportunity to get to know and speak to Mr. Bensadoun. He recommended that I go to school for international business.

After that trip, I walked into my school counselor's office to tell her that I wanted to go to the University of Illinois at Urbana-Champaign (UIUC) to study international business. My counselor was not helpful and was very discouraging, this is why it is important to have mentors. My mentor was a lively and determined Puerto Rican lady from New York, who believed in me and knew my capabilities. She helped me to complete my college application to the one school I was determined to attend, UIUC. And to my surprise, I was accepted. I was enthused, but then reality set in. How was I going to pay for it? If I moved to UIUC, that would mean I would have to leave my job, and I would not be able to help my mother. Given my circumstances, being a first-generation student and the first in my entire family to attend college, savings for my college was not existent. Luckily, my mentor helped me to complete scholarship applications, which covered my tuition and room and board. I also worked during the summers.

During my time in college, I took full advantage. I was on the dean's list, co-founded the Central and South America Student Association (CSASA), became a proud member of Alpha Psi Lambda National, Inc., and I met my future husband there. And, to satisfy my international business requirements, I studied finance in Hong Kong, China and Granada, Spain. To afford these study-abroad experiences, I attained a paid internship with a life insurance and financial services company as an underwriter. This was my introduction to the industry.

Soon after I graduated, I became a district manager with a top payroll company, but not without some convincing on what I, as a Latina, could do for them. At my interview, the regional manager walked in with a look of confusion. He saw me and then quickly glanced down at my resume. At that time, I went by Evelin Flaherty, having taken on my stepfather's last name. At that moment, I assumed he was expecting to see a young white, educated bilingual woman, in fact, he questioned my last name. Although I had already had two phone interviews that said I was qualified, he began to give me excuses as to why I would not be a good fit. I instantly gave him examples of how my life experiences have prepared me to not be fazed by the word "no" and the rejections that a sales representative experiences on a daily basis.

I was ready! I was coachable, a quick learner, and had the heart—and still do! He was impressed that I did not take "no" for an answer and he gave me the job. I began my first corporate career making six figures, with a company car, a company computer, and a company phone. When you are the first of many, having these company essentials meant more than it should. A year later, I purchased my first home, where my primary bathroom was bigger than the one-bedroom apartment I grew up in. Mama, I made it. *¡Lo logramos!*

Shortly after that, a good friend in his mid-twenties was in a car accident, which resulted in a coma. All of his family and friends rallied around him, took turns staying at the hospital, and planned a fundraiser for him. I saw first-hand how this tragedy impacted his family, not only emotionally but also financially. A couple of months later, a close family friend, also in his twenties, was found dead in New York. He left behind a grieving mother and children. Again, not only was the family impacted emotionally but also financially. These two tragedies changed the trajectory of my professional life; I felt a calling to educate my community on the importance of life insurance and long-term care insurance, to prepare them financially for any unexpected tragedies, like the ones my friends' families had just experienced. I decided to change careers to a profession where I could have a positive financial impact on families. But my family questioned, how could I go from a six-figure salary to 100 percent commission after so much sacrifice and hard work? My answer was easy, our communities deserve more. I was no longer choosing a career for the money but rather following my new personal mission.

That first year in the industry, I broke a record in the Chicago North Shore office, insuring the most families in one year, thus winning the Community Impact Agent of the Year Award, Career Life Success Award, Career Life Producer Award, Career Life Achiever Award and the Life Foundation Award. Yes, I was impacting my community, and everything aligned with my mission. Then reality set in; I took a huge pay cut that first year. So, I decided to broaden my business model to include investments. I enrolled in courses to attain more licenses: the Investment Company and Variable Contracts Products Representative Qualification Exam (Series 6), the Uniform Securities Agent State Law Exam (Series 63), the Securities Industry Essentials® (SIE), the Uniform Investment Adviser Law Exam (Series 65), the General Securities Representative Exam (Series 7), and more professional designations. I also earned my master of business administration (MBA) degree. I am a strong believer in being a lifelong learner.

As I grew with the company, another obstacle arose. I was made to believe being a woman and planning a family would hinder my financial success. I listened, and I declined the offer to be the first Latina partner in the Midwest, for a successful, almost 200-year-old financial services company. While attending one of my first partner training meetings, I looked around and noticed I was one of only two women in a sea of male colleagues. Here I was, at a national partners training meeting in Plano, Texas, feeling so proud, knowing I deserved and had earned this moment. As the meeting continued, the speaker turned to us women, "remember that the first years of this career are going to be a lot of late hours, and no time off. So, if you are planning on having kids, don't worry about missing any of their early milestones since they would not remember their first three years anyway." I went from sheer happiness about having made it this far to a feeling of shock and sadness. I didn't want to miss my children's first milestones. After having discussed this with my husband, I quickly realized I would need to make a difficult decision and decline this prestigious opportunity. Initially, I was resentful, but soon after motherhood began, I knew I had made the right decision to commit to my family. In the midst of this, I learned to believe in myself, which led me to much more success than I could ever imagine and the understanding I can really have it all. You really can. I turned my six-figure annual income into my monthly income. You can, too.

I went on to open my own financial services company, Mastermind Wealth Strategies, LLC, during the COVID-19 pandemic, while I was pregnant with my third child. Being a mother was no longer an obstacle, and nothing was impossible. Despite being in a male-dominated industry, my first year in business I was inducted to the Million Dollar Round Table at the Top of the Table, recognized in the Negocios Now 40 under 40 Class of 2020, and named in Forbes Top Best-In-State Financial Security Professionals in 2022.

For many years, I lived with the belief that I was not good enough, which had been instilled in my mind by my father when I was a four-year-old little girl. That belief has completely vanished! I now get to help families not live paycheck to paycheck or borrow from one to pay another. Instead, I help them plan for their futures and have financial freedom, because that is what our communities deserve. That is what my mother deserved.

I learned that I can serve others best when I am prepared and actively decide to fully lean into my life's mission. I am grateful for all of my life experiences and know that everything in my life has happened for me, not to me.

MY FINANCE INSPIRATION

It is no secret that Latino buying power is rapidly rising and fueling the economy. With that being said, it is important to have Latinas in finance careers supporting our community with their financial decisions. It's time. You can help your clients build generational wealth. This is important not only for our community, but also for ourselves. So, improve on your craft every day, whether it's formal education or certifications, and always strive to know more. Work on yourself. If you grew up believing that you can't make money because you don't have the right connections, the right background, etc. know that it is just a limiting belief, change your mindset and be a lifelong learner.

To my fellow Latinas and women who read my story, if I could come from a broken home, not knowing the language, and at one point homeless, to now owning multiple homes in multiple states, turning my six-figure annual income into my monthly income, by simply following my passion of creating financial literacy in my community, then you can, too. Understand your finances. Surround yourself with mentors and coaches that have already accomplished what you want to accomplish, so that they can help you reach your goals faster. Write down your financial goals, look at them every day, and know that you can have it all. Just believe in yourself and take action today! A book that I highly recommend is *Think and Grow Rich* by Napoleon Hill. It can help you think bigger than your limiting beliefs, not only for yourself but also for your clients. See you at the Million Dollar Round Table.

BIOGRAPHY

Evelin F. Freytas is passionate about education and financial wellness. She voluntarily facilitates educational workshops and personal education sessions for the Money Management Educators Network (MME). She is the first woman and first Latina/o in Illinois to be a part of MME, a not-for-profit organization that partners with many of America's leading corporations. Her common-sense approach to the otherwise complex world of personal finance is what makes her a sought-after educator.

Evelin has been active in the financial services industry for thirteen years. As the founder and CEO of Mastermind Wealth Strategies, LLC, she helps individuals and business owners reach their financial goals by creating a financial roadmap. Her career is built on the premise of assisting her clients on all things with a dollar sign.

Evelin earned her bachelor's degree in international business from the UIUC and she received her MBA in Chicago. Additionally, she studied finance and international business in Granada, Spain, and at The Chinese University of Hong Kong in China. She received her CLTC®, FSCP®, and LUTCF® designations through the American College of Financial Services. She holds Series 6, 63, SIE, 65, and 7 licenses.

She has been inducted into the Million Dollar Round Table, Top of the Table; and received other honors, including Negocios Now 40 under 40 class of 2020, and Forbes Best-In-State Top

Financial Securities Professionals in 2022. She is president of the Ecuadorian Volunteers Association (EVA) and former president of the University of Illinois Latina/Latino Alumni Association (LLAA). Most recently, she became a national ambassador for the Grief Sensitive School Initiative (GSSI).

She is happily married to Dr. Héctor Freytas, a high school principal, and they have three sons: AJ, who is five years old; Carmelo, who is three; and Romeo, who is one.

Evelin F. Freytas, MBA, CLTC®, FSCP®, LUTCF®

Efreytas@mastermindws.com

www.mastermindwealthstrategies.com

Facebook: @EvelinMastermindWS

LinkedIn: mastermindwealthstrategies

LIZ QUINTANA-ROMERO

"Seeing my parents accomplish things like homeownership and real estate investments molded me into making that a priority for myself."

I'd like to say that I knew exactly who I wanted to become since day one, but I would be lying. I had no idea what I wanted to be at a young age. What I do know is, I sure didn't believe in my full potential. Growing up as a first-generation Latina in the United States felt like a maze trying to figure out life. To this day, I'm still learning new things that my parents didn't know about either. We are new to this country, and despite being born here, it's important to remember to not be so hard on ourselves. For those of you who are like me, first gen, we are the first to finish high school, first to graduate college, first to obtain certain careers, first to invest in stocks, first to buy a home. We are the first of many things in our families, and we have so much to be proud of. We must give ourselves a round of applause each time, small or big accomplishments, because we are the ones who are making it all worth it for our parents.

My people are *gente humilde;* we have reasons to be. We come from nothing, and still don't have everything. But we are grateful, and we keep striving for greatness. If you're struggling with finding the industry in which you want to serve, you might gravitate towards what you know. You might think some things aren't for us or they just seem so far out of reach. At least that was my case. I remember growing up being asked what I wanted to be when I grew up and always having a hard time defining a career. Everything seemed so far out of reach, like it was impossible. Women who looked like me, who were new here, weren't represented as much in certain careers. When I thought of a mortgage banker as a teen, I automatically thought of a bank and an old Caucasian man, characteristics I can't relate to. I grew up on the East Side of Aurora, Illinois, near my favorite place to be after school and summers, Phillips Park. Growing up I remember barely seeing my father because he worked long hours. I always think about that when I see my siblings enjoying him at a young age. I'm grateful that I get to spend so much time with him now. I grew up a single child until I was in the seventh grade, and my beloved sister came along. "My mamas," even though I'm much older than her, she is the one who keeps me grounded whenever I'm too hard on myself. Six years later my baby brother, Panchito, was born. Having siblings has been one of my greatest purposes. The love I have for those two is the same love a mother has for her children. Being a big sister in a Mexican household means a lot of things. It means being a babysitter, driver, tutor, and even a third opinion on making decisions in younger sibling's lives. If you can relate to being an older sibling, you know the amount of pressure it brings to be a good example for the younger ones. Being the eldest made me more driven to show my siblings that no matter what happens, we must go after what truly makes us happy. We must try it and have no regrets.

I've realized as I get older, I am a lot like my mother. She, too, is the oldest sibling, who had to help raise all her siblings. She even had to work to help provide for them at one point, something I didn't necessarily have to do. My mother told me the story of when they immigrated to the United States from their hometown of Santa Maria La Loma, Estado De Mexico, Mexico. Both my parents decided to immigrate here to give me a better life. My mother tells me her father used to come and go with a work permit, but my mother felt horrible as the eldest sister seeing her family separated. She is the oldest of seven siblings. She begged her father to bring her along to work to save up money to help to reunite her family. I share all this because I admire her strength as a woman. My mother didn't have much of a childhood because she had to grow up so fast to improve her family's situation. My mother and grandfather were able to save enough to unite the family and to apply for citizenship. It wasn't easy. When they got here, they had little to no money. No car.

No English literacy. Both my parents struggled. There were times they walked to work, experienced difficulties learning their way in a new country and a new language. My parents had a rough start, but they didn't let that stop them from achieving better. My mother always told me their story of how they only rented for one year when they got to Illinois. My mother disliked living in an apartment building. She sat down and set up a financial plan to cut down expenses, budget, and save more to be able to buy. With both of my parents' hard work and determination, they bought their first home after a year of renting. They were only twenty-three years old. My mother has always been my drive, she speaks with so much passion and emotion that she makes me feel her stories when she tells them. I admired them for these accomplishments. I always knew homeownership was valuable and necessary at a young age, because my mother embedded that in me. Saving and doing well with money isn't about how much we make, but what we do with it. Sure, making six figures is ideal, but no matter what we earn, if we don't budget or save to invest it, we are on the same cycle. It's just a bigger check going to a bigger bill. Knowing how to balance our finances is so important. As I continue to grow, I realize that who I am is what my parents showed me. Seeing my parents accomplish things like homeownership and real estate investments molded me into making that a priority for myself. As a child I didn't know who I wanted to be. I knew I wanted to be like the people I admired in history class, people like Martin Luther King Jr. and Dolores Huerta. But most importantly, I wanted to be like my parents, who started with nothing but managed to give me everything. I've learned that with difficult times come great things. During the year of the lockdown due to COVID-19, I did a lot of thinking. Outside of binge-watching Tiger King, baking with my sister, and going for morning runs, I thought deeply about my purpose in this world. I reflected on who I am and what I value. I am who I work on, day in and day out. I help families like my parents, who start by renting but want to achieve homeownership, whether that is a month from now or in the next few years. I help people like me, who didn't know a lot about what opportunities are out there; I show them what they can do. Homeownership is so much more than having a mortgage and firing your landlord, although that is amazing. It means owning an asset, growing your income with equity that builds over time. It's creating generational wealth you can pass down to your family. It's allowing yourself to be debt free if you're open to paying off your home to reinvest in something else down the road.

I remember early on dreaming of having my own home. Something about having ownership of a home, and being able to say, *I did this,* feels right. The first home I bought was one that I chose after only seeing four houses in the same neighborhood. I was an easy homebuyer to work with, but I wasn't picky for a reason. I went in knowing my first home wouldn't be my forever home. You see, early on, I made the decision that I would invest in real estate.

My generation has owned the idea of being an entrepreneur. We don't have to choose anymore; we have mastered wearing multiple hats. Now, I know why I never knew what to say as a child what I wanted to do when I grew up. It's because it wasn't just one role. It was many. I'm only getting started. There are so many ideas and ventures I want to pursue that I can't wait to tackle them. Up until I was a sixth grader, instead of crushing over boys with my girlfriends I was cutting up old clothes that no longer fit me and turning them into something fabulous for my Brat Dolls. To me, it was always the easiest way to express myself without saying much as a first impression. I love the idea of showing who you are and how you feel by what you wear. This year, I decided to finally stop fantasizing and make it real. I've always dreamed about having my own boutique. So, I will soon launch my small online boutique where I get to help women with tools, resources, and style to achieve greatness. The truth is, we are the only ones who set rules for ourselves. We can accomplish so much. The key is, we must start somewhere, because if we don't start, we will only take longer to live up to our fullest potential. This goes towards everything, chasing what makes us happy, becoming a homeowner. We must start somewhere and continue to work our way up. My father once said, people who wake up tired and hit the snooze button do so because they forget to find their why. We all have a reason that drives us to be excited about the opportunity we have each day to live. This is true. Finding our why is important because every day isn't easy or successful. Some days are hard, and we feel like everything is falling apart. We must not forget our why. To all my fellow Latinas, Latinx this chapter is for you. I hope that my mother's bravery pushes you to keep going, that when you have many dreams like I do, that you plan on how you will achieve them. For those who sometimes feel like they are alone or want to give up, I encourage you to remember the battles we all fight, and that life is meant to be tough. So, live up to your fullest potential, with confidence, a good planner and a cute outfit!

MY FINANCE INSPIRATION

1. Why choose finance? It's important to have people in our own communities offer financial services. I think it's important to provide these services in our communities for those who need it. I love being able to change someone's life in a big financial way. It means I am helping families begin generational wealth. This is one of my whys.

2. I encourage anyone reading this to try whatever it is that interests you. It is okay to change what you want to do. There are no rules. You get to decide what makes you happy and what your purpose is.

3. For anyone interested in learning about mortgages, or anything else I may be a resource for, call or text me anytime.

BIOGRAPHY

Liz Quintana-Romero is a mortgage loan officer in a top-producing office. She enjoys meeting new people who are ready to achieve homeownership and getting them to the closing table. She also enjoys buying investment properties and is working to grow her portfolio. Liz works on building her online boutique, House of Queens Boutique, LLC, where she can be creative. Her goal is to empower women and uplift them with the clothes and tools she offers. Liz is also a podcaster. On The Ambiciosas Podcast, she discusses relevant topics, featured guest speakers, and much more. Liz also is working on other projects with the Hispanic Regional Chamber of Commerce in her community for the youth.

Liz Quintana-Romero
MyHouseOfQueens@gmail.com
Facebook: Lizeth Quintana-Romero
Instagram: @iamlizqueentana, @Lizgivesloans
@HouseofQueensL
TikTok: @Lizgivesloans

WARRIOR

CYNTHIA BELTRAN

"The good or bad experiences we lived shaped the person we are today."

THERE IS GOOD IN EVERYTHING IF WE ARE WILLING TO LOOK FOR IT.

I am a proud Ecuadorian and Latina woman. When I repeat this, I feel empowered. It has always been essential to me not to lose the identity that makes me who I am. I came from a third-world country and grew up in a middle-class family. As a kid, I was creative, sassy, and not too dedicated in school, but I always had the urge to learn something new. Since I was little, I always saw life with some humor that really make a difference in my life no matter what. There is always a reason to smile.

My parents divorced when I was a young teenager, marking

my life. My mother was a strict woman with a strong temper. My dad left the house when I was young. When I became an adult, I understood my parents better.

There is a story behind every person, and a reason behind every action. My dad never lived with his mom; my mother also had rigorous parents. I still get sad when I think about that. When I think about my mother, I know her life purpose is to help others. She is a genuine woman with a golden heart. She serves the community as a mission in her life. She is also a woman with incredible resilience. She will always keep her chin up no matter what she faces.

My father has always been calm and affectionate with his kids and a hard worker. I decided to keep the best from both of them.

CHOOSE TO BE GRATEFUL

My family was plentiful. I was the third of four kids, plus aunts, uncles, cousins, and friends nearby. It was so lovely to have so many friends and family around; there was never a dull moment. Most days in Ecuador are sunny and warm; I do miss those days. I didn't realize how blessed I was with that weather all year long when I lived there.

I no longer take sunny and warm days for granted in my beautiful Chicago. In Ecuador, we had the privilege of having a person who helped with the cleaning and daily cooking, but my mother always taught us to be humble and appreciate what we had.

Sometimes as parents, we think that giving our kids the best is the right thing to do. The reality is, that thanks to not getting everything I wanted as a kid, I appreciate everything I have now even more. I am glad they didn't raise me to be selfish and think only about myself. When I was a kid, we shared meals, clothes, chores, and toys. As an adult, I know sharing is an enormous act of love.

I know that hard work will always pay off. The good or bad experiences we lived shaped the person we are today. I am a decision-maker and warrior, and when I need to close chapters, I will do it to open new opportunities or new beginnings. I love to help people, but more than anything, I am a woman of faith. When we are with God, everything is possible.

EVERYTHING YOU NEED IS ALREADY INSIDE YOU

God wants us to live in abundance, not in poverty, but we must work for it. I learned that if I know how to manage money, work for my goals, help others, and be grateful, the rest comes by itself. I decided to use the bad experiences to be better. I chose to challenge myself and never stop.

My financial journey started when I was about ten. I used to call kids in my neighborhood to teach ballet classes. I remember writing in my notebook the names and payments made. My little sister, Katherine, had no money to pay for the lessons then. She was always on my "deny list" of no fees paid (hahaha). Since I was little, I have thought that business is business; we always remember this and have a good laugh about it. As a teenager, I was very responsible. I have worked since I was sixteen. I went to high school and then worked in the afternoons. As soon as I finished high school, I started studying English. I always understood I wanted a better life. "One day, I will be able to help others." I would repeat this over and over when I was a kid. "One day, I will have a big house, a lot of money, a big family, and travel worldwide."

THE PAIN, THE JOY, AND THE LEARNING

I came to the United States twenty-two years ago. It was the country of dreams. I remember walking on a famous street, Ocean Drive, in Miami Beach. I was staring at everything like a kid opening her favorite toy. It was a joyful moment. I felt the ocean breeze, the people were happy, and the whole picture was unreal. Everything looked perfect. I stayed there a few nights before I went on to my destination, Chicago.

Thanks to my stepfather, Fernando, my mother decided to move to the United States. He was an extraordinary man. I won't ever forget him. I can't thank him enough for giving me this opportunity and for all his support while he was alive. I was only supposed to visit for a few months. But after seeing the beautiful clean streets, the kind people, the stunning architecture, and the great opportunities, I knew this was my chance to make my dreams come true.

After having over ten different jobs in three months, I struggled to find myself working in restaurants or doing the same thing every day. I started working in a cell phone store, and then took a job as a secretary in a dealership. A few months later, they offered me the salesperson position. I was terrified. I had to switch from hourly pay to commission. I took the challenge, and sometime after I got promoted to store manager. The following eighteen years of managing were stressful and required demanding hours, but every day was a challenge. I had to set goals and train people to achieve their goals, and my favorite part was helping others reach their potential. My store was number one for consecutive months and years. The owner, Ranny, saw my potential, and I can't thank him and the company enough. I never gave up on his business, and he never gave up on me.

Whoever has worked in sales knows that money is unlimited. That's why I could start with my investment properties. Instead of buying luxury cars, jewelry, clothes, or technology I saved money to travel with my son and invest in real estate.

LEARN FROM YESTERDAY, LIVE FOR TODAY

In 2004, I got pregnant with my firstborn, Stefano. He forever changed my life, perspective, priorities, finances, and goals. He inspired me; I started saving and putting my finances in order. I kept 20 percent of my salary in savings. I saved money for investments, traveling, buying a house, and opening a college account. My son gave me that boost of energy to do everything. My dream was to travel the world with him. The finances were great, but I knew I had to work hard to make all these things happen.

I started going to college again because I wanted to make my son proud. I wanted to pursue my financial freedom so he would never have to suffer for money. Still, I realized that not everything was about creating good wealth for my family, because in my journey to make everything right, and thinking about creating the best financial situation for my family, I lost my marriage. My son's dad, Eduardo, is a great man, but we married young. We needed to learn how to balance, how to prioritize, and how to learn to make things work. We were also very different, overall. We separated, and then we divorced.

My heart still cries when I remember all the time I was away from my son for the demanding hours of my job. But I lived and learned. Eduardo and I have an excellent friendly relationship, because we decided that working together was in the best interest of our child.

TAKING RISKS OPENS UP NEW OPPORTUNITIES

In 2004, we bought a luxury townhouse with an adjustable-rate mortgage loan, which meant that the interest rate changed after a few years. The recession came in 2008, and our mortgage went up in 2010. The townhome was worth a lot less. I wish someone had explained why I should not have signed up for that type of loan when I bought that house. It was a big mistake. But I did not know better then. In 2012 we sold our beautiful townhouse in a short sale. We went back to renting for two years until we figured out how to find our way separately. I felt devastated, losing the house that my son loved and the family we had formed. I was losing all hope at that moment.

The market went down, and in our worst moment, we decided to invest all our savings in a cash investment property. That was the best decision ever. We had to move again as the landlord had lost the house in foreclosure. I decided to buy a house with little savings, credits from the seller, and a good credit score. That is all. I was able to buy a two-flat property. My bank account was at zero, but I had my own house again for my son and me.

Time was running out. I divorced with nothing in my account. I owed a debt to my ex-husband, and I had $30,000 in debt on credit cards, as well as an investment property to fix. I moved to a new house, and I lost my job. I never went into bankruptcy, even when the divorce lawyers recommended doing so. I decided I didn't want to have that on my credit rating. I got into those debts, and I had to pay them. I took what I learned, and I made the impossible possible.

A POWERFUL MIND CAN ACHIEVE ANYTHING

I started creating different ways to make money. I never stopped paying for my son's college account and my life insurance. I worked and worked and worked some more. I went back to work at the same dealership to be able to pay for all these debts. Before I noticed, God gave me another chance. Not only did I put my life in order, but also my finances and my personal life. I met my partner and lovely husband, Francisco. I was still paying debts for a few more years. I was always reading about how to get out of debt and to recover from a financial crisis. Reading is a powerful tool that I am still developing.

I paid all my debts. I started saving again. We kept moving forward. Francisco and I believe that self-growth is the key for us to live fulfilling lives. Knowledge is a powerful tool. I like to be around positive people, and he is always learning something. We encourage ourselves with our potential and help each other with our weaknesses.

My husband and I, before we met, always wanted to have a big family. Be careful what you wish for; it may come true. We are a happy big, blended family; Stefano, my step-kids, Vanesa and Mateo, and Julieta, our daughter; they all keep our lives very active. They are the most meaningful reason we want to be better every day.

After failing the test three times, I got my real estate license; the third time was the charm. I have been a happy and busy real estate agent since 2020. I am an investor and have created passive income through the years with real estate in Illinois and Ecuador. But more importantly, I have found my balance in life, and I am just getting started.

MY FINANCE INSPIRATION

Surround yourselves with people that help you be better.

Persistence removes resistance.

Always find your why.

My advice is that you never stop following your dreams.

Always find balance in what you do.

Do not take anything for granted.

God changed my life forever, and He can change yours.

I recommend these books:

Rich Dad Poor Dad by Robert Kiyosaki

The Alchemist by Paulo Coelho

BIOGRAPHY

Cynthia Beltran is a Latina who is proud of her roots. She was born in Quito, Ecuador, and moved to the United States in 2000.

Cynthia is a persistent woman with a strong character that has led her to exemplary achievements. She managed a car dealership for eighteen years, where she was able to mentor and help others reach their best potential. She has a degree in marketing management and social science. Cynthia is an enthusiastic woman that has always loved to help others and working with people is what she likes the most. She finds her passion in real estate. She is a real estate agent and investor who has been able to create a portfolio and passive income through properties in Illinois and Ecuador.

Cynthia forms part of The National Association of Hispanic Real Estate Professionals® (NAHREP) Events Committee and volunteers her services in the Care Center of Willowcreek. She is a woman who knows that she can always find something good in every experience, and is a positive, cheerful woman who believes in constant development.

Cynthia is a happy wife, proud mother of Stefano and Julieta, and proud stepmother of Mateo and Vanesa. Her inspiration and excellent support come from her kids, parents, siblings, lovely friends, amazing clients, and her beloved stepfather, Fernando.

Cynthia continues being inspired by her mother's heart and strength, but more than anything, she feels immensely blessed to be a woman of faith.

Cynthia Beltran

cynthiabeltran.realtor@outlook.com

Facebook: @CynthiaBeltranRealtor

Instagram: @Cynthia_Beltran_Realtor

HOW I GOT AHEAD OF THE GAME

RUBI VELAZQUEZ

———

"Push the envelope, own your path to financial freedom. As for me, the people I care about have been directly impacted by my career choice."

We are trained to suffocate money, stunting its growth. Money carries its own energy, and if we do not put it in places where it thrives, we will stunt its growth. It will never reach its full potential. Without the understanding of giving back, we fail to help its flow.

There are many facets of me: Family woman, mother, professional, businesswoman, and legacy maker. As I share, I hope to inspire a vision of what your facets look like, leaving encouragement to shape the world. Leave your footprint everywhere you go. Your name, your actions, and your bravery speak before you do. Do not take it for granted.

ROOTS

My life began in Mexico. My mom was born in Tecalitlan, the heart of Mariachi music development. Yup, I am a Mariachi fan!

My dad was born in Michoacan, the host of the best Day of the Dead celebrations, amongst many other notable historic events, and where Hidalgo performed El Grito de Dolores.

My grandparents started their life in Zapopan, Jalisco, known as the home of the Virgin of Zapopan. The population makes it the second largest city in the state, behind Guadalajara.

I was born in Guadalajara, Jalisco. When I was eight years old, the United States became my new home.

HOW THIS LIFE SHAPED ME

I appreciate the four pillars of life that make a human successful: health, family, money, and spirit. My parents' greatest legacy was teaching us not to be afraid to start new, even if it means leaving something that makes you successful in just one pillar.

By the time my father hit his thirties, he had served as the bodyguard of several presidents in Mexico. He had served in the military before becoming a bodyguard. This came at a cost; he realized the lifestyle he provided for his family only covered one pillar. He made the bold decision to leave a well-paid job, a great position in the public eye, for the future of his family. He passed away knowing he did all he could to provide for his children, in the best way he knew how.

My mom, on the other hand, had a gift of healing to humanity. She was a "Curandera," which means a witch doctor. Those who got a "no" from the medical industry came to her for alternative answers. She gifted many families with her healing gifts. I went to home appointments with her when I was a child. My siblings and I were blessed to experience the results of her expertise. She was unlike any woman I have met. Faulty, but good. At her funeral, I recall waves and waves of people introducing me to their new family members which doctors said could not exist, or healed humans who claimed they were here because of her. Ma found her gift at a very young age, this gift carried her everywhere she went, when we moved to the United States, this kept her mind, body and spirit alive while she walked this earth.

They traveled to the United States (known as "El Norte" in Mexico) to take a job at a factory.

We had a military lifestyle at home. We were all soldiers, there was no room for the weak. We had to be strong, no matter what life threw our way.

We moved to the North Side of Chicago, near Wrigleyville. Not long after, we moved to the Pilsen area, then to Little Village, where we stayed the longest.

HOW DID I END UP IN FINANCE AND HOW DID IT CREATE A FUTURE FOR ME?

I remember the times in my life as if they were points on a timeline. I was eight years old, then sixteen, nineteen, twenty-three, twenty-nine, thirty-five, thirty-nine, forty, and I am still growing. As I think back on all the stages of my growth, at the age of nine I recall studying people and money, how it was utilized along with time, energies, and resources. I measured the results of it. At the time I was not aware financial skills would be my gift to society. Funny thing, in the back of my mind I thought I was going to be a psychologist. I thought I understood humanity. But my true gift was understanding the language of business, and the world of accounting.

My home was not a place for a child. I had gang member friends, and enemies—everything in the ghetto. I felt confused, so I went to the library. I kept my mind occupied. I learned to keep things to myself, understanding this world was sketchy and unpredictable. I was a nerd growing up in the ghetto looking for my space in this world.

Time and love collided. At the age of sixteen, I was pregnant, and of course I had choices like those available to any other girl living in the ghetto: abortion, giving up children, becoming a mom with or without a partner. I wanted to make a new opportunity in life. I decided to be the best mom and role model, no matter what it took.

Years passed, and I taught myself many things. I was curious and hungry for a good life. I learned the value of saving, investing, and multiplying my money. I was seventeen years old when I learned about credit. I took finance and accounting in high school as electives. By the time I was nineteen years old, my credit score was 850. I did not tell anyone, and I was happy. Doing the homework, I knew that was not going to be the end. It was the beginning.

I learned to be a young professional adult. I took myself on an education journey. At the age of twenty-three, I registered at DeVry University. I took care of my health. Diabetes scared me as it had taken my mother's life. I was a single mom, and I had a full-time corporate career. I graduated when I was twenty-eight years old, coming out with a family, no longer a single mom. It took five years of part-time schooling, in the evenings and on weekends. I achieved something no one believed I could do.

A few years later the real estate market crashed, and everyone was filled with fear. I lost my corporate position as an accountant, human resources and payroll master. This was one of the scariest times of my life; I had never been in this situation.

Four months later my mom passed away. I became a mess at this time. I felt lost, like everything I did was for nothing. I chose a new mantra: life's a b^&* and then you die.

I realized I could be a mess while growing. I could learn, make mistakes, and not be stuck! I have always been fearless and resilient, so why give up now? I went back to my past goals to pick up the missing pieces. I came across an important one. When I was twenty-three years old, I had written down: "Become a financial advisor."

I had found my next career path as a financial adviser and business owner. I went through an intense training with the corporation I represented at that time. I studied day and night, skipping outings. Preparing to take on six different tests: four insurance licenses and two investments designations (the Series 6 and 63), I did everything in my power to talk to potential clients by October 2014, and by my goal date I was sitting with clients, advising, insuring, enforcing credit, and diversifying investments to multiply money using compound effects. As I continued to develop and work with more clients, I was amazed at the lack of education among the masses.

I decided to take my education into my own hands again, connecting the dots. I started to learn about stocks, real estate, digital coins, private funding, hedge funds, and bonds. It was required to advance them as I was advancing myself.

Time passed, and it happened again. I realized I was not living the life I wanted. I was away from my children more than I wanted to be. It was time for a change, and times did change. Good and bad things came my way during this realization. It was like the universe pushed me again towards another whirlpool of life. Slight thought came: "It is time to bet on yourself." I went to school specifically because one day I wanted to be a business owner.

I had been doing taxes on the side every tax season since 2006. My sophomore year I took a tax class and the instructor said: "You are now qualified to do taxes." So, I did. I was nonchalant about it; I was doing it for the experience, while creating another stream of income.

In 2016, I took inventory of my skills. I opened multiple new businesses, separating my new streams of income, I began to set structures and systems in place to bet on myself. I launched MRV Financial as my main source of income. This had to work!

It did work, though I soon found that it was hard for

people to get it as I decided this would be a virtual company. As a young student, I studied at home, and I learned how to work from home, so that I could be with my daughter. I only went to school to exchange homework with my teachers or take exams. It was natural for me to think of the virtual concept, but my systems where questioned. People were accustomed to my office in downtown Plainfield, Illinois, which meant I had a new problem to overcome. I stayed consistent, ignored the negativity, focusing on activities towards growing my virtual financial firm of accountants and financial advisors. I was ahead of the current trend and mindset, and this pushed me to keep going.

In December 2019, we started doing weekly money-themed YouTube videos, and we continued to release newly researched content based on the need.

When the pandemic hit in 2020, I was three years as the CEO and founder of MRV Financial, with the support of my loving husband. I had employees trained, and systems in place. My business blew up! The pandemic validated my organization, and it said to others, I knew what I was doing. I received more yesses! I could not have seen the future, and I prepared for it as if I could.

The tax rules changed during this time; it was extremely hard to keep up. Many businesses like mine closed their doors— CPAs, RAs, accounting firms, etc. I had already taken my shot, and now I ran with it. I could not fail.

Fast forward to today. I have built many income streams. I am part of business joint ventures. I sit on the executive board with NAHREP Chicago, and other smaller boards, aiming to close the Hispanic wealth gap in the United States. I continue to look for ways to educate and give back to our communities.

I am here because I believe in me and the power of people, by the numbers. In the success of consistency, focus, and resilience.

Finance is not a career. It is a legacy, a path, and an opportunity to give back to our family, friends, colleagues, and communities. Through finance I give others the opportunity I created for myself.

SETTING THE 'MONEY IS EVIL' RECORD STRAIGHT

I believe in giving to those who cannot help you. I volunteer to humanitarian causes. This is one of the legacies I would like to leave behind for generations to come. I have been blessed to be a philanthropist with causes I care about.

In case you have been led to believe money is evil—money is not evil. God needs us to be wealthy, in all areas of our life. If we do not have it, how can we help those in need? Money is a reward for giving our expertise to this world, through our labor and resources. The more we utilize our gifts to improve the lives of others, the more lives we impact. I encourage learning the laws of money and seeing it through a different lens.

MY FINANCE INSPIRATION

Push the envelope. Own your path to financial freedom. As

for me, the people I care about have been directly impacted by my career choice.

Repeat this mantra: "I make intelligent decisions, which lead me to financial freedom."

More than ever, Latinos are a large group in the United States. According to the 2021 Census Bureau, the Hispanic population was 62.6 million, or 19 percent, of the nation's population. Finance is broad. Our knowledge and application affect decisions made daily on all parts our life. Education in the proper, useful, and correct path to wealth advancement is needed.

TOOLS AND RESOURCES

These weblinks could help you to grow:

Investopedia.com: A financial tool covering all aspects of finance serving as a financial dictionary from insurance, forming a company, credit, and investing.

Creditkarma.com: Stay up to date with your credit. While not accurate on points, you can catch trends and public financial information about you.

BIOGRAPHY

Rubi Velazquez is a financial advisor, accountant, and business owner. She holds a master's degree in finance and accounting. At the time of this publication, she is a certified public accountant (CPA) candidate at the American Institute of Certified Public Accountants. She is CEO of her own company, MRV Financial.

Rubi is always looking for ways to serve and invest in her community, and surrounding communities as well.

As a financial advisor, Rubi has been helping people to set financial goals and to achieve them since 2014. Once hired, Rubi drafts a plan for her clients. She has access to different investment types and is able to help her clients to choose and to make sound decisions. She helps them to diversify their investments and align them toward the goals she helps them to set.

She worked in various accounting jobs before opening her own business. She is someone they can talk to who can provide professional information.

Rubi also helps people in her community to achieve their goals and to make their dreams of financial freedom come true.

Rubi Velazquez
Mrvfinancial.com
(815) 556-9629
Advisor@mrvfinancial.com

CHANGING THE FACE OF THE
FINANCIAL SERVICES INDUSTRY

CRISTINA
PINEDA

---

*"It was crazy for me to entertain the idea of going back
to school, to get more into debt, and try to get a job which
wouldn't even pay me enough for the lifestyle I had, just for
me, a one-person household."*

In late 1979, my parents, my brother and I immigrated to Chicago, Illinois in the United States from Tiripetio, Michoacan, Mexico. I was not yet two years old. We lived in Little Village, a predominantly Mexican immigrant community, and we worked hard. My mother stayed home to raise us while my father worked for La Zenith (Zenith Electronics, LLC), a company that manufactured televisions. The pay was not great, but at least it had good benefits. It was a reliable job with a 401(k).

My father did not want my mother to work or to learn how to drive. That was not what married Mexican women did. I was told to go to school, to get good grades, and to earn a college degree so I could get a good job with benefits, to get married, to buy a home, to work for forty years, and to retire. Sound familiar? My mother would say to my sister and I: "Get a degree, 'una carrera,' just in case. If your marriage doesn't work, you can go your way."

When I was four years old, my mother decided to get a part-time job. She did this against my father's will, of course, but she wanted to start contributing to our household. My mother had big financial goals, and dreams for our family's future. She believed that the people we surround ourselves with, the people we listen to, are vital. They shape who we become.

My mother's first boss, a very hard-working Mexican immigrant man, had just opened his family-owned business in the heart of our neighborhood. He advised my mother to save money to buy a house and to live in a better neighborhood with a better school system.

On July 11, 1984, my sister, Claudia, came into this world, completing our family of five. Shortly after, we became legal residents. In the spring of 1987, my parents became proud owners of a two-story building in Cicero, Illinois. Finally, the American dream was becoming a reality for us. At times, both my parents worked full-time jobs and part-time gigs, here and there. I can still hear my mother's stern words: "Get good grades, get a degree, get married, and then you can do whatever you want." At last, la candaleta started changing, so I took that and ran with it. My goal was to graduate college, not so much to get married, but don't let my mom hear that. I wanted to become independent! I wanted to move out, maybe get married, because, you know, that's what good Mexican daughters do. Then I could get a good job downtown and, eventually, go into business for myself. All that could come true. But life had other plans.

La Zenith, where my father had worked for over twenty years, announced its closure due to filing Chapter 11 bankruptcy. Bankruptcy, como? That wasn't a word the Mexican community liked to hear nor are they used to it. Zenith gave its thousands of employees two options: They could retire early or get a two-year technical degree to start a new career. But before they announced this, and it was just a rumor, my dad did not want to wait to be let go. So, he turned in his resignation. His dream had always been to move back home to Michoacan, Mexico. He didn't want to be one of those immigrants who just dreamt of one day retiring after working hard forty-plus years and then not making it alive to retirement. "Eso no es calidad de vida," my dad would say.

While my parents planned the move, I graduated from high school. I had no clue what I needed to do to help our family make a smooth transition. I didn't even know if it made financial sense to move. I did not feel the confidence to get into a four-year university. I didn't think I was smart enough and, I thought, we didn't have the money or resources. Whether those were limiting beliefs or just stories I told myself, it somehow comforted me staying local while most of my friends went away to college. Staying local, in my comfort zone, meant that I could work full time and go to school full time, and still help my parents monetarily with any challenges that might arise for them. I started classes at a local community college.

My father chose to retire early. He withdrew his 401(k) vested funds before 59 1/2 and sold our primary residence. Wait what?! You mean my father didn't know about the early withdrawal penalty fee and taxes?! No, he sure didn't. He didn't know about the three rules of money. Where would he have learned those from? He was a working-class, blue-collar employee. The three rules of money are how to accumulate money, how money grows, and how money gets taxed. They are information that the wealthy, 5 percenters in this country pay the financial giants to help them create generational wealth, live financially free, and leave a legacy to their heirs. The 95-percenters, like my parents, relatives, friends, and communities are not going to pay to obtain this information. They are overlooked by the traditional financial giants in the industry as they do not have the net worth they require.

We moved to Mexico in the spring of 2000. Due to lack of financial planning, I had to move back to the United States and finish my degree while I worked full time as a teller at a bank in downtown Chicago. I signed off on multiple student loans. As I had promised my parents, I graduated from Robert Morris University in July 2004 with a bachelor's degree in business administration with a concentration in accounting. Mother, Father, I did it! Now, I could go do whatever I wanted. I had worked so hard to earn this degree, I was ready for that good-paying job, and the financial security and benefits that came with it. I went to human resources and asked what the protocol was so I could apply or advance to a better paying position within the bank. I knew those student loan payments were coming and living off my teller's income was not going to be enough. The HR director advised me to go to my manager and ask her to refer me to an opening as soon as she knew of one. OH BOY! That didn't go too well. I will never forget that day. I did as the HR director advised and asked to meet with the branch manager. The branch manager went off on me. "Who do you think you are," they said, "coming in here thinking you're going to climb the corporate ladder overnight? Who cares if you now have a degree? There are people working here that have been here way longer than you, ten-plus years, and they, too, have degrees. Take a seat and wait for your turn. The way you go about things just leaves a bad taste in my mouth."

With a lump in my throat, I said okay and walked out. As an immigrant Latina already filled with limited beliefs, lack of self-worth, and fear of advocating for a promotion or salary increase, this was devastating for me. I found a staff accounting position at a construction firm then gave two weeks' notice. I called the HR director to process my exit interview at the bank, but within fifteen minutes, the bank's chief financial officer (CFO) called and asked me to meet with her immediately. I asked the branch manager for permission to leave early and was told that I didn't have to stay and comply with the 2 weeks' notice, that I could leave at that moment. I felt very disappointed. I wondered how many other women of color and minority had been treated this way here. I vowed never to forget where I came from and to always help others in need and in my reach.

I met with the CFO of the bank and was offered an internal audit liaison position right on the spot. It was a position they had just created, and I was to develop it. Did I mention that I was going to make almost double in pay from being a teller. Guess who called me to offer me a position at her branch. Yes, you guessed it, the branch manager who said I couldn't climb the corporate ladder overnight! The CFO took me under her wing and mentored me. I was promoted to audit officer on my one-year anniversary. Wow, I couldn't believe it. Less than two years after graduating college, I had an officer position, making $50,000 a year plus bonuses, health insurance, three weeks paid vacation, six federal holidays off, six sick days per year, and the famous 401(k). For years, I did not know how my 401(k) worked but I contributed to it by default, just like my dad did. I wish someone would have told me that I could design my own retirement plan. Did I mention that I was able to buy my very own first real estate property?! At twenty-seven years old, I bought a condominium. I was an unmarried woman and it stated that in my closing documents when I bought my condominium. All I wanted was a home of my own, so that when my family needed it, they'd have a place to stay. Owning a condo was one of the greatest feelings in the world for me as a young immigrant single Latina. I learned so much and acquired many valuable skills throughout my time in that audit position, starting from the CFO to the internal and external auditors, state and federal examiners, and board of directors. The CFO was a middle-aged Caucasian woman, very classy, kind-hearted, hard-working professional, a shareholder and the only female on the board of directors of the bank at that time. I am forever grateful to her for believing in me and hiring me for that position.

In early January 2009, I was called into a meeting. "Effectively immediately, we have terminated your position. You have thirty minutes to leave. Here's your severance package details and unemployment benefits folder. Do you know how this works?" I could only think to myself, no I don't, why would I? I am Mexican, we don't use those. I was that girl in the sitcom scene, being fired, walking out of the building with my plant and personal belongings.

I was unemployed for two years while the country recuperated from the 2008 recession. I could not find a job. I was either overqualified or underqualified. It was crazy for me to entertain the idea of going back to school to get more into debt and try to get a job which wouldn't even pay me enough for the lifestyle I had, a one-person household.

Then, I was introduced to one of the largest and fastest growing leadership development business platforms in the financial services industry. It was changing the face of financial services for women in the United States of America—women of all races, colors, backgrounds, and ethnicities. What an honor and privilege it was to have the opportunity to become an independent business owner. I work for myself, but not by myself. I got paid to do what I loved on my own terms. People don't plan to fail, but they fail to plan. I educated and served our communities; I especially focused in areas where we were overlooked by the financial giants in the industry. By the way, it was 95 percent of people in our hard-working communities. I taught financial education, and I did it for free.

In January 2022, I celebrated my ten-year anniversary in the financial services industry. I now am focusing on leadership development, producing more independent agency owners in underserved communities across the United States of America. I am changing the face of the financial services industry, one Latina at a time!

MY FINANCE INSPIRATION

I chose finance because my family did not have the proper financial education, resources, and tools to make better financial decisions as we grew up. Seeing my father go through financial devastation made me realize how many people are in a similar predicament. Here is some food for thought:

"Americans can expect to inherit $72.6 trillion over the next quarter century, more than twice as much as a decade ago," according to a Bloomberg news report published February 2, 2022.[11]

"The biggest wealth transfer in history is about to happen. This Great Wealth Transfer is about to kick into a higher gear.

---

[1] https://www.msn.com/en-us/money/markets/tax-f ree- inheritances-fuel-america-s-new-73-trillion-gilded-age/ar- AAToZS1#:~:text=Tax

As much as $68 trillion will change hands between various generations over the next twenty-five years," according to a CNBC report published October 21, 2019.

"I predict that half of financial advisors will be gone in the next ten to fifteen years," said Ric Edelman, founder of Edelman Financial Advisors in the CNBC report.[2]

It's not a matter of IF something's going to happen, it's a matter of WHEN, and when it does, are you financially prepared?

The following are a couple of books I recommend:

- *Secrets of the Millionaire Mind* by T. Harv Eker
- *Money. Wealth. Life Insurance. How the Wealthy Use Life Insurance as a Tax-Free Personal Bank to Supercharge Their Savings* by Jake Thompson
- The Power of Zero documentary by David McKnight https://www.youtube.com/watch?v=qlr9kvBNptQ

[2] https://www.cnbc.com/2019/10/21/what-the-68-trillion- great-wealth-transfer-means-for-advisors.html

BIOGRAPHY

At the age of twenty-two, Cristina Pineda realized that most of her family challenges at that time were due to financial stress. Lack of financial planning was the number one factor causing her family to disintegrate. Every one of her family members needed to find a way to financially survive.

In her job as a bank teller, Cristina started to notice the lack of financial education in the Latino community. It wasn't just her family, it was most people, in various professions. Cristina observed that most people didn't know the basics of budgeting, saving money for unexpected emergency expenses, saving for their kid's college, planning for retirement, or protecting their ability to have an income, in case they couldn't work due to an illness.

In 2009, Cristina was forced to make a career change. She knew she wanted to be a part of the solution and have control of her time, money, and freedom, all while helping her Latino community. In 2015, Cristina became a senior broker at World Financial Group Insurance Agency. She became a six-figure-earner by June 2016. In January 2022, she celebrated having her own financial agency, being a bilingual Mexican Immigrant, and being a Latina financial professional for over a decade.

Cristina Pineda
CristinaPinedaWfg@gmail.com
(708) 369-0019

ABOUT THE AUTHOR

Imelda Rodriguez is the founder and CEO of Coaching Vida, LLC. She created the company to provide the necessary tools to obtain a better lifestyle through holding seminars, courses, workshops, and conferences, as well as one-on-one and group coaching sessions (life and financial coaching) that she named Coaching Vida (coaching life).

She is also founder of the Entre Nosotras Talk Show, a video blog that has been live for more than ten years revolving around women's supporting topics. Imelda is also credit as asset master trainer of the Credit Builders Alliance, among many other certifications that support her work.

In June 2021 she received the Latina Community Spirit Award from the Latinas Voice Awards. As of May 2017, Imelda became a contributing author of Today's Inspired Latina Vol. III. She possesses many key leadership qualities and is passionate, persistent, direct, optimistic and creative, hard-working, enthusiastic about building relationships, open to feedback, and energized towards developing people to their fullest potential. She has shown true perseverance and dedication to her work and dreams and has a true belief in people and the power of change.

Imelda exhibits a commendable and courageous willingness to self-reflect, to adapt, to negotiate, and to try new and different things to build her leadership capacity. She intentionally sets ambitious goals for herself and her teams and has accomplished much in the lives of the clients she serves.

Throughout her work, Imelda has remained committed to multigenerational legacy and implementing homeless prevention services to reduce emergency situations that lead to homelessness or crisis. She deeply believes that we can be the best version of ourselves and we can grow and develop our greater purpose and impact through learning. Her own growth as a leader in her community and in her businesses is the greatest testament to the deep and powerfully transformative truth of that belief.

The best is yet to come!

Imelda Rodriguez
CoachingVida21@gmail.com

Imelda.innovacion@gmail.com
(312) 912-3222 and (312) 694-5364
Facebook: @CoachingVidaFinances
Instagram: Coachingvida2020
LinkedIn: @coachingvida